A WORKING MAN'S *Guide*

STRONG VALUES, STRONG LIFE, STRONG LEGACY

DR. MARK L. TEAGUE, PHD.

MT Squared Publishing, LLC
teaguesix@yahoo.com

Scripture quotations taken from the (NASB®) New American Standard Bible®, Copyright © 1960, 1971, 1977, 1995 by The Lockman Foundation. Used by permission. All rights reserved. https://www.lockman.org/

S&P® and S&P 500® are registered trademarks of Standard & Poor's Financial Services LLC, and Dow Jones® is a registered trademark of Dow Jones Trademark Holdings LLC. © 2024 S&P Dow Jones Indices LLC, its affiliates and/or its licensors. All rights reserved.

Library of Congress Control Number: 2024911143

ISBN: 979-8-9907371-1-2 (paperback)
ISBN: 979-8-9907371-2-9 (ebook)
ISBN: 979-8-9907371-0-5 (hardcover)
ISBN: 979-8-9907371-3-6 (audiobook)

Ordering Information:
Special discounts are available on quantity purchases by corporations, associations, and others. For details, contact teaguesix@yahoo.com.

Publisher's Cataloging-in-Publication Data
Names: Teague, Mark L., 1964- , author.
Title: A working man's guide : strong values, strong life, strong legacy / Dr. Mark L. Teague.
Description: [Abilene, TX] : MT Squared Publishing, 2024. | Summary: Presents a plan for the class of men who are working: starting with principles of problem-solving and covering how to apply these principles to deal with stress, family relationships, and public policy, to achieve success and restored vitality.
Identifiers: LCCN 2024911143 | ISBN 9798990737105 (hardcover) | ISBN 9798990737112 (pbk.) | ISBN 9798990737129 (ebook) | ISBN 9798990737136 (audiobook)
Subjects: LCSH: Working class men. | Men – Conduct of life. | Problem solving. | Stress management. | Success. | Marriage. | Parenting. | Faith. | BISAC: SELF-HELP / Personal Growth / Success. | SELF-HELP / Self-Management / Stress Management. | FAMILY & RELATIONSHIPS / General.
Classification: LCC HQ1088.T43 2024 | DDC 305.31 T--dc23
LC record available at https://lccn.loc.gov/2024911143

This book is for the American working class. May you ever be strong and prosperous. And stop listening to politicians. They loathe you, manipulate you, and steal from you and your great-great yet-to-be-born grandchildren. Take charge and own your existence. I wrote this book for that very purpose.

Contents

LEGACY CONSIDERED

MOST WANT TO live a life of significance. Far fewer give consideration to what this means or requires. This writing intends to provide insight into the meaning and requirements of a significant life for the common, average workaday fellow. This book speaks most directly to the male gender, although I sincerely hope females will benefit from both the information and the intended effect upon males at large. Ladies can at least study the principles and be more able to direct the males under their care, a task for which only a female is forever and always suited. If all goes as intended, we will be more worthy of female companionship. The male gender is forever in debt to our better part, the female gender, for they keep us from self-injury.

Legacy, simply defined, is what you leave behind. Just a few generations back, legacy, both figuratively and literally, meant an inheritance, some material item left for one's heirs. The meaning has progressed in modern times to have a more general application.

Like it or not, aware of it or not, our life is a legacy in the making. It may be broad and well known, which is rare, or it may be narrow and last a short while. Nonetheless, a legacy will be left. Our life, our interactions, leave a lingering tale with those around us. What will it be? How will that tale be told? What will it say? Let us explore what a committed believer in Our Lord and Savior should consider as he makes his way through this uncertain, chaotic, oftentimes unfriendly, and hostile world.

The reader of this work may be at various points regarding their view of faith, Eternity, and a Divine Being. The range can be from edged atheist to curious skeptic, quiet and private faith to boisterous, joyous expressions of religious belief, and all points in between. All persuasions of belief are welcome as you enter these pages. The stance of this writing and its author is that of a lifelong, deep, tested, and committed faith as taught in the Holy Bible. The hope and intended outcome of this work for the unbelieving or doubting reader is clear insight and understanding in how a person of faith attempts to navigate daily realities through this life. The hoped-for outcome of this work for the committed believer is encouragement, sharpened understanding, depth and breadth of skill, and a heightened passion for engaging in daily life with a vibrant, sustaining faith in the Almighty. In both cases, believer or skeptic, may this writing provoke thought and consideration to the question, in the words of the great Francis Schaeffer, "How should we then live?"[1]

ABOUT ME

My wife, Melissa, and I were high school sweethearts. We grew up together, went to the same community church, had common

---

[1] Francis A. Schaeffer, *How Should We Then Live? The Rise and Decline of Western Thought and Culture* (Wheaton, IL: Crossway Publishing, 1976).

circles of friends, and enjoyed shared experiences from early on. We even have a picture of me at her second birthday party! Yes, at two years of age! It's one of our very favorite photos, and we display it with warm memories and affection in our home.

Ours is a very traditional, old-fashioned American story. We've been married almost 40 years now. We raised four kids and currently have nine grandkids—and are hoping for many more!

We grew up in north Texas, the Texas Panhandle, on family farms. Farming and ranching were huge parts of our community and how we made our living for several years. In the mid- and late-1980s, after we got married and started a family, the farm economy was tough. Cash flow was tight, and we decided we needed to change our livelihood.

As every person and couple will realize at some point, it is hard to have a home without a livelihood. Through that decision process, we concluded that graduate school would give us the most options. In today's world, you gotta have skills. The more skills you can add, the more options you will have, and the better chance you will have of success.

The key idea was just that: options. You never know what tomorrow holds—you cannot know, in fact—but you can do things now that will give you opportunities and open doors. So, driven by this fact and economic circumstance, we went to Oklahoma State University, where I earned a doctorate through the Department of Agricultural Economics.

Toward the end of my studies, we faced another important choice, another fork in the road: go into academia or industry? We put a lot of thought into making that decision and decided industry was our best way forward. So, Melissa and I took the industry path and found success in banking and finance. That decision shaped our careers and set our course for almost the next 30 years.

The last leg of our banking and finance path was a 10-year stint with a private equity group in Houston, Texas. Toward the end of this phase, Melissa and I started a manufacturing company, producing small-arms ammunition. When you grow up on farms and ranches, firearms are an everyday part of life.

During my banking career, I had taken up competitive shooting as a hobby. This led me to start reloading ammunition, given the volume of ammunition fired and special load requirements. I spoke often with Melissa about going commercial with ammunition manufacturing in retirement.

As our kids got older, especially when the youngest got her driver's license, Melissa came to me and said, "I have more free time now. I would like something to do. What do you think I should do?"

We discussed several ideas, and along the way I said, "Well, we could start an ammo business." I was mostly joking, and I figured she would say, "There's no way in heck I'm doing that."

Lo and behold, she thought it over a minute and said, "That's perfect. That's exactly what I'm looking for." And we went from there. Melissa worked full-time, and I worked evenings and weekends to get our business up and running.

Melissa was the founder and president of Lone Star Munitions. After wrapping up in banking and finance, I joined her full-time for a couple of years. We have now sold the company and entered retirement.

Being able to look back has allowed me to consider our experiences through life and what it's meant to find a path, to build a family, and to do something good in this world. The principles I've outlined in this book have helped me—and I hope they'll help you create and build your own legacy, to leave something behind and do something good in this chaotic, oftentimes unfriendly world.

It's my firm belief that the working class is the lifeblood, the strength of the United States—if the working class does well, America does well. If the working class struggles, America is weak. America has always been a working-class nation. And the working class should not be defined by income. A literal definition is best—the class that is working.

Some think entitlements are the answer to working-class decline—that is a lie, or at best, wishful thinking. Entitlements create dependency and dependency is a cancer. A cancer that kills us slowly and surely. Look around you. We see the effect everywhere, every day, and it should shake us right to our core. Just take a look at the official U.S. Labor Force Participation Rate report (Appendix, Figure 11).[2] We should be terrified of what we see.

Free this, free that, government this, government that. Nothing is so expensive as when you ask the government to make it free.

The biggest fib from the entitlement crowd is that we are forced to build a welfare state so we can have a social safety net. Another lie—this one isn't even wishful thinking. There are good, strong, persuasive arguments in favor of building a social safety net, even a broad, deep, thorough one. Nothing in those arguments links inherently to entitlements. A proper, healthy social safety net, even a big one, especially a big one, will be based on ownership, not entitlements.

Humans respond to incentives—that is a basic, hard fact. If we incent hard work and ownership, we will get hard-working owners. If we incent entitlement status, we will get complaining, whining, snot-nosed slugs and brats asking for everything under the sun. Again, take a look around you. What do you see? What are we becoming?

---

2   "Civilian Labor Force Participation Rate," U.S. Bureau of Labor Statistics, accessed February 7, 2024, https://www.bls.gov/charts/employment-situation/civilian-labo r-force-participation-rate.htm.

We face some key choices as a country. The national debt forces the issue. We try avoidance as an answer, but it runs short on time. What I can do now is speak clearly and forcefully to what Melissa and I have embraced—the type of lessons and values that have helped us live a fruitful and happy life.

I hope to be a voice pointing us in a direction that is both ancient and modern—you can have both roots and wings. America can hold to sacred traditions, time-honored values that work, while also crafting and pursuing a vision for the future. Melissa and I have lived it—old America in a modern world—and we know it works.

HOW TO APPROACH THIS BOOK

This book is meant for working-class males of any age, anyone from the teenage years, when you start picking up your first job, or you start dating, somewhere in there, all the way through to the end of your life. However, if I do my job right and reach my goal, that working-class male will be living with purpose, and there will be a spillover effect to the people around him. The ladies involved in this working man's life should enjoy and benefit from the material as well.

I will refer to that working-class male as Working Man. We need to get to know each other. We will spend many pages together as we work through this topic. Let's get on a first-name basis!

The intent is to make you, Working Man, more suitable for the working-class female. Because there's just no substitute for family. Family is the eternal, matchless, building block social unit. We see all kinds of family failure, but when marriages fail or falter, people go right back to it. Folks marry again, maybe again, maybe a bunch of times, retreat to children, parents, the cousin that actually understands them. Everything goes back to that family unit—because there's no escaping it. It is irreplaceable.

Family needs to be upheld and honored. It is a sacred institution. This book is built on that value.

I will hereafter refer to the working-class female, with deep and great respect, as Working Woman. We need to get to know each other as well, but most importantly, Working Woman, I hope you get to know and think more highly of Working Man. That's the real point in all of this. If I can make him more attuned and suited to your needs, I have succeeded.

Life is hard! It is difficult in a lot of ways. A steady stream of problems will inevitably come your way. But you can step through all of them and be successful in the end. Life will rid you of your naivety, strip you down to basics. If you can see that, if you are in the middle of that, if you want to help those around you walk through that, this book is for you.

I'm hoping to help those who see the value in tradition and wonder how to apply it in a modern world, those who see past trendy fads and value the deeper ideas, the foundational ideas, things that can form a bedrock for life. For those who appreciate themes and logical patterns, ideas rich in history, something of substance, this book is for you.

It's kind of a fad these days, this thinking that everything traditional is evil, or at the very least out of date and no longer relevant. For anyone who thinks that—anyone who's into politically correct trends and wokeism—this book probably isn't for you. Offense awaits you on every page. That kind of thinking, these modern, faddish ideas, cannot deliver and they are at best a distraction. At worst, they are complete lies. Lies that take people down a bad path that will not fulfill, does not satisfy, and is empty of meaning.

There's a strong moral base to what I say in this book, but the thing I can say—loudly and clearly, and now in my sixth decade—is that this works. Every idea you read here is tried, tested, and personally lived out over many years. And for a Working Man who wants to learn strategies that work, things that can help you through this difficult thing we call life, I think you'll get a lot out of this book. This book is most definitely for you.

And, Working Man, if you care about helping that lady friend of yours, the Working Woman who might possibly share a lifetime with you, if you can convince her, this book is a must read. You might even have her read it first and then tell you what to do. That could be just the ticket.

Be warned. The views expressed herein will often run counter to prevailing cultural notions, and that is the entire point. A legacy defined by bowing one's knee at the altar of modern culture is not a legacy worth leaving. Let us proceed.

Chapter 1

PRINCIPLES OF SUCCESS

COMPLEXITY CONQUERED, STRESS RELIEVED

LIFE COMES AT you in a relentless, unforgiving way. A series of problems emerge, one followed by another, and another, and another still. Pessimism is justified, although hope remains right at hand.

Spiritual hope abides as an enormously powerful idea and gives a believer eternal comfort through every pain. A believer knows that death will certainly end this physical life, but also that this is just the beginning. Eternity picks up from there, Eternity secured by promise, a promise upheld by our Savior.

How to adjoin these spiritual facts with practical, everyday living? What brings the Eternal Hope of Christ into the family's monthly budget? What allows a young married couple to rear children and keep any miter's measure of sanity on an hour or two of sleep per night? What joins Eternal Hope with a middle-aged worker now unemployed, with serious concerns about income, skill set, competitive advantage, family obligations, and the basic point of this burdensome life?

There exists a daily tension, a conflict, between hope and trouble. Hope is always available, and trouble is usually at hand. Pay attention, Working Man. This one is important. It will define you, shape you, reveal who you are.

There's really only one path through this tension, only one that works, a path that creates what you want and builds a legacy worth leaving. It's the path that will make you the man you should want to be. It's the path that will give Working Woman the man she needs and deserves. There are many alternatives available. In the end, they all fail. They are fakes, deceptions, and have a bad end. Only one path gives the desired end. Walk with me, Working Man. Let's talk it through. Let's explore how it can be done, day by day, step by step.

We will never be free of problems as long as our heart is beating, there is breath in our lungs, and we tread upon this earth. Understand and accept that life in this present world is nothing but a series of problems. To think otherwise will bring frustration beyond measure—and worse. The one who engages in effective problem-solving has a solid chance to get something done. Nothing guaranteed, mind you, but a solid working chance to build something worthwhile. The one who does not try, the one who doesn't bring to bear basic abilities granted to us by our Maker, will be buried under a pile of problems. This one will suffer loss.

Our Maker has not left us in despair. Let's explore a tool, a very powerful framework, which not only makes this difficult life manageable, but also makes it brim with hope and opportunity. When mastered and applied with a steady hand, the results are stunning. Divine, in fact.

Imagine a problem as an amorphous, shape-shifting blob. Life comes at you that way—undefined, unwelcome, often without warning. It is threatening and overwhelming. That last visit to the doctor's office may have been shattering, or the next. You never know. The news of an unfaithful spouse brings emotion and strain, which cut deep. The acts of a child who was raised to know better and had every opportunity to behave better bring a burden that no parent wants to carry. Picture Figure 1 as circumstances, potentially bringing uncertainty, risk, damage, and loss, with no end in sight.

If you allow your circumstances to remain an amorphous blob, threatening you daily, hope fades, despair becomes the norm, and joy is nowhere to be found.

But there is a different approach, one sanctioned by the Almighty. This approach does not deny the difficulty of life but changes entirely our actions in its midst. Take this same problem, this same blob, and frame it. Place a structure around it, give it definition.

Once you establish a frame, you can take action to solve it. Rational, logical, systematic, definitive action. Problem-solving. The world is now a better place. Let us explore this option and discover the secret.

Take the same image from Figure 1, a threatening blob, and apply structure. Here is what we get:

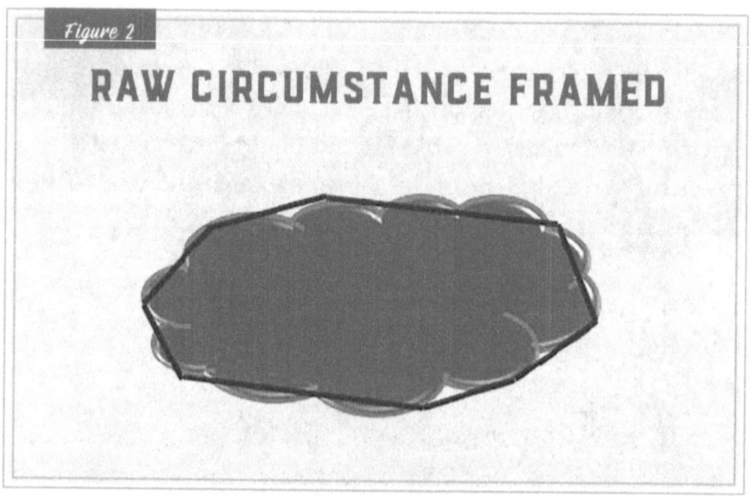

Don't work against the blob. Work against the frame. Yes, it takes practice. Yes, you will make mistakes. Yes, you can get the frame wrong and reach wrong conclusions, maybe taking wrong actions. You may even have to start over—many times. What better things do you have to do? Cry and whine? Act like a victim? Check out and quit? Blame somebody? Disappear into addiction or bitterness and anger? Get over yourself and get busy. You have work to do.

Figure 2 is manageable. Figure 1 is a threat, an impending loss. The difference between the two is not circumstantial—the surrounding events and frustrations remain the same. The difference is our response, using the tools the Almighty has given us versus victimhood. We have a logical, rational mind. We have experience. We have time, energy, abilities, and ideas. These are gifts from our Creator. He expects us to use them. Each of us has the obligation and opportunity to make the world around us a better place.

The method described above is generally known as the scientific method. Take a problem, small or large, frame it, and work systematically and logically against the frame. The frame is known as a theory, if you care for the academic term. This can become formal, including serious academic rigor, but that isn't necessary for everyday application and success. The more you practice this in daily life, the better you become. Problems are no longer overwhelming and threatening. The initial shock of a new problem can still be unnerving, but you have your method, your approach, your habit. Frame it, break it down, and solve it a step at a time.

The concept should be clear, Working Man, and don't panic over the how-to side of things. I won't leave you suspended in the land of the hypothetical. We have two concrete examples at the end of this chapter, and the entire remainder of our conversation is about applying this problem-solving approach to essential areas of life. You will be very capable and equipped when we reach the end of our talk. Here are some key points about the problem-solving approach:

- Problems are coming your way, whether you like it or not. You do not have a choice in that matter. However, you get to choose how you respond, how you handle them. There is great power and effect in that choice.

- A problem is immediately reduced to an addressable issue by a reasonable frame. If you can capture 70% or more of an issue in a logical framework, you can break it down and create solutions.

- Adjust the frame using experience and knowledge. You get better at it with each trial. With practice, you can get that capture rate up to 90% and higher. Seasoned old-timers speak with confidence for a reason: they've seen trouble before.

- Never—I repeat, *never*—allow problems to bunch up or blend together. This is an old and favorite trick of the enemy of our soul. If you allow four or five problems to bind as one, it becomes unsolvable and overwhelming.

- If you make the mistake of allowing four or five issues to conglomerate and seem unsolvable, Working Man's typical response is simply to be angry, all the time. If you happen to be in a relationship with our better counterpart, the Working Woman whom you are very fond of, guess who bears the brunt of your anger? Yes, she does, and at no fault of her own. Discipline is required, so remember: the components are solvable, the conglomerate is not.

- Accordingly, while you are applying a frame, or even before you start, be sure to break a problem down into separable components. Frame each part and address one at a time.

- Once separated, prioritize the issues. Normally, only address the top one or two, three at the most, and then move down the list. Everyone has resource constraints. Time, energy, money, and patience are not unlimited. Live within your means, including when problem-solving— especially when problem-solving. Don't spread your resources too thin.

- If you are facing a problem and find it difficult to create a working frame, you have most likely failed to separate issues, as described above. Break a problem down into its basic units and frame each one separately.

- If difficulty in finding an appropriate frame for a particular circumstance persists, trusted counsel is in order. A seasoned and experienced outside view can be of high value. Be cautious and choose this counsel wisely. This modern world is full of garbage advice steeped in self-centered thinking. If self-referential sentiment forms the core of any counsel, wisdom will not find you.

Create the habit described above, and you have the Working Man's version of the scientific method. You do not need a laboratory or an academic appointment. You have the best lab in the world: everyday life. As you live this way and form this habit, you will discover an amazing secret: complexity can be conquered and stress relieved. You can always handle a couple of stress items well. Do not let them bunch up and don't freeze when the amorphous blob shows up at the door. Frame it, break it down, and take action. Listen, learn, and repeat. This is a good way to live, my friend, living life to the fullest, with passion and purpose.

This tool, when practiced, puts you in possession of the same strength used by the greats of our past, the folks that changed history: Thomas Edison, Jonas Salk, Cyrus McCormick, George Washington Carver, Johannes Gutenberg, Alexander Miles, Alexander Graham Bell, and countless others, known and unknown. The difference between Figure 1 and Figure 2 is the difference between improving quality of life and constant human misery. Master the technique. Make it your own. The tool is not selective of the user. It is available to anyone caring to try.

Use what God has given you to make each day better and more wholesome, and aspire to a higher quality of life. Accept life for what it is and serve God every day with a whole, open heart. That is faith and it is pleasing in His sight. He tells us that plainly in His Scripture.

THE POWER OF PRINCIPLES

The believer has an enormous advantage in this life, too often not availed in the course of daily living. We are endowed through the Holy Scriptures with the knowledge of principles, and not just of any kind, but principles revealed from Heaven by the Almighty Himself for the benefit of His children. The Creator of Life and the Universe grants insight into the structure, the workings of daily affairs. Why would we not use this knowledge? By all means, we should.

Principles give us a foundation upon which to stand, a mooring to hold us in times of storm. Principles are the difference between chaos and poise, anger and deliberation, purpose and a life adrift. Christ said it best:

> Everyone who comes to Me and hears My words and acts on them, I will show you whom he is like: he is like a man building a house, who dug deep and laid a foundation on the rock; and when there was a flood, the river burst against that house and yet it could not shake it, because it had been well built. But the one who has heard and has not acted accordingly is like a man who built a house on the ground without a foundation; and the river burst against it and it immediately collapsed, and the ruin of that house was great.
>
> Luke 6: 47–49

Live as a disciple or learner of Christ. Read His Word, consider it, and live by it. Learn the principles and use these to create the logical frame outlined above. Make it an everyday exercise in problem-solving.

Without reference to principles, the problem-solving demanded by daily life is slower, much more difficult, and far more prone to failure. Principles serve as a toolbox, a means from which to draw knowledge to build your frame. With repeated use and the constant replenishment and addition of principles to your toolbox, you become a master.

Life is now transformed from an endless series of problems to each day renewed with hope, joy, love, and faith. Rather than stressed, pained, and angry, you become a man of God, filled with hope and optimism. This life is temporal. Make the most of it. Do all the good you can. Using principles to frame problems and solve them is an outstanding way to live.

As mentioned above, the results are stunning. The master builder of frameworks for problem-solving can only be a person steeped in principle. They will constantly seek knowledge and underlying themes, for they constantly seek better tools. They understand the challenge of life and they desire to be adequate to the task. Their reward is materially significant and well earned.

The human condition is vastly enhanced through a commitment to and application of this scientific, principle-based problem-solving methodology. Technology, medical science, business methods and process, economic conditions, and quality of life are all vastly improved by steady application of logical, rational problem-solving. Take a seemingly unsolvable problem, break it down, frame it, and create solutions. This works in a laboratory, in a large company, in a university, and it works profoundly well in your normal, everyday life.

The person without principles, or the person who refuses to use them, essentially has an empty toolbox. Good luck with that Figure 1 problem when it shows up.

Take a different approach, Working Man. Be bold, be confident, and use the tools God has given you. Fill your mind with principle, themes, the deeper ideas of life. Learn to build your problem-solving framework quickly, accurately, and efficiently, and then problem-solve at every opportunity. This world is given to us as a temporary home. Let's make it better.

MY PARENTS' PRINCIPLES

I must give credit where it is due—my parents gave me a great foundation of deep and sound principles to live by. They taught me well. They poured their heart and soul into me and my siblings. They provided us with a base of values and beliefs through which to process decisions. They provided the guidance and instruction, and as I matured, I adopted these values as my own.

There were many lessons and points to absorb, but three main points stand out. These three got the most attention, the heaviest emphasis. They taught me, with consequence, if I chose not to listen:

- Be honest

- Work hard

- Show respect

They hammered these principles home in a big way, and they have never left me.

EXAMPLES

We have established the idea of framing life's problems based on principle. Now, let's review some concrete examples, one historical and one relational.

Communications Technology

The day was January 8, 1815. The place was roughly 5 miles southeast of the French Quarter in New Orleans, in what is now Chalmette, Louisiana. The United States Army under Major General Andrew Jackson met the British Army, led by Lieutenant General Sir Edward Pakenham. The result was a clear American victory: British withdrawal, just over 2,000 British casualties, American casualties of 333, and the elevation of Andrew Jackson's reputation in electric fashion, leading him to the presidency of the United States of America.[3]

For the near 2,400 soldiers, American and British, who incurred death and the injury of battle, the resulting loss and suffering to families should have never occurred. The War of 1812 was formally ended by the Treaty of Ghent, signed on December 24, 1814, 15 days earlier, but word could not reach the battlefield in time. The treaty was signed in Ghent, Principality of the United Netherlands, now in Belgium, so with the available communication methods of the day it took at least a month for the message to reach New Orleans.[4]

To state it mildly, communications technology has changed since early 1815. Today, a message would fly to Washington, DC, and all related parties at near the speed of light. The impact of improved communications on related events, if available in 1815, is obvious,

---

[3]   Matthew B. Dale, *The Staff Ride Handbook for the Battles of New Orleans, 23 December 1814 – 8 January 1815* (Fort Leavenworth, Kansas: Army University Press, 2015), https://www.armyupress.army.mil/Portals/7/educational-services/staff-rides/ StaffRideHB_NewOrleans.pdf;
John S. Brown, "British Suffer Heavy Losses," *Army Magazine*, 65, no. 1 (January 2015);
Robert V. Remini, *The Battle of New Orleans* (New York: Viking Press, 1999).

[4]   William Earl Weeks, s.v. "The Treaty of Ghent," in *The Oxford Encyclopedia of American Military and Diplomatic History* (New York: Oxford University Press Inc., 2013);
Donald R. Hickey, *The War of 1812: A Forgotten Conflict, Bicentennial Edition* (Urbana, IL: University of Illinois Press, 2012).

positive, and profound. The suffering of widows, orphans, family loss, and human carnage would never have occurred.

Consider the challenge for a moment. In 1815, how could a person or message travel some 4,800 miles across the Atlantic Ocean from Ghent to Louisiana in anything less than a month? It was unthinkable, unheard of, impossible, a Figure 1 problem, to be sure. This unsolvable blob, a threat to daily life, carried significant and in some cases severe implications for all involved. It was a problem without a solution, or so it seemed at the time. Hundreds of thousands of individuals facing hundreds of thousands of problems each day accepted that communications were slow and bound to geography. That was everyday, on-the-ground reality. What happened between then and now?

Let us turn a moment to another story and follow it in parallel. This story begins April 27, 1791, with the birth of Samuel F. B. Morse. Born in Charlestown, Massachusetts, Samuel Morse received education at Phillips Academy and Yale College. He developed as a painter and was in Britain for study and work for the entirety of the War of 1812.[5]

For all participants of the War of 1812, and certainly to those at the Battle of New Orleans, the answer to better communications was on its way—they just did not know it yet. Morse and a few colleagues developed the single-wire electromagnetic telegraph. In 1832, 17 years after the Battle of New Orleans, Samuel Morse met Charles Thomas Jackson. Mr. Jackson was knowledgeable and active in the study of electromagnetism. While discussing several experiments in electromagnetism with Mr. Jackson, and combining that with his own prior knowledge of electricity, Samuel Morse developed the idea of a single-wire telegraph. From this work came the original Morse telegraph, which now sits in the

---

[5] Carleton Mabee, s.v. "Samuel F. B. Morse," *Encyclopedia Britannica*, last modified December 19, 2023, https://www.britannica.com/biography/Samuel-F-B-Morse.

National Museum of American History, part of the Smithsonian Institution.[6]

Working Man, listen to a few quotes and experiences from Morse himself, drawn from his letters and personal conversations:

> I think you will not complain of the shortness of this letter. I only wish you now had it to relieve your minds from anxiety, for, while I am writing, I can imagine Mama wishing that she could hear of my arrival, and thinking of thousands of accidents that may have befallen me, and I wish that in an instant I could communicate the information; but three thousand miles are not passed over in an instant and we must wait four long weeks before we can hear from each other.[7]

This quote by Samuel F. B. Morse is accompanied by a note added by the editor of Morse's letters, Edward Lind Morse: "On the outside of this letter written by Morse in pencil are the words: 'A longing for the telegraph even in this letter.'"[8]

Here is a summary by Edward Lind Morse of the initial immersion of Samuel Morse into the relatively new field of electricity:

> In the year 1827, Professor James Freeman Dana, of Columbia College, delivered a series of lectures on the subject of electricity at the New York Athenaeum. Professor Dana was an enthusiast in the study of that science, which, at that time, was but in its infancy, and he foresaw great and

---

6   Kenneth Silverman, *Lightning Man: The Accursed Life of Samuel F. B. Morse* (Cambridge, MA: Da Capo Press, 2004); Paul J. Staiti, *Samuel F. B. Morse* (Cambridge, UK: Cambridge University Press, 1989).

7   Samuel Finley Breese Morse, *Samuel F. B. Morse, His Letters and Journals*, vol. 1, ed. Edward Lind Morse (Boston: Houghton Mifflin Company, 1914), 41.

8   Morse, *Letters and Journals*, vol. 1, 41.

beneficial results to mankind from this mysterious force when it should become more fully understood. Morse, already familiar with the subject from his experiments with Professor Silliman in New Haven, took a deep interest in these lectures, and he and Professor Dana became warm friends. The latter, on his side a great admirer of the fine arts, spent many hours in the studio of the artist, discussing with him the two subjects which were of absorbing interest to them both, art and electricity. In this way Morse became perfectly familiar with the latest discoveries in electrical science, so that when, a few years later, his grand conception of a simple and practicable means of harnessing this mystic agent to the uses of mankind took form in his brain, it found a field already prepared to receive it.[9]

"If the presence of electricity can be made visible in any part of the circuit, I see no reason why intelligence may not be transmitted instantaneously by electricity."[10]

Here is a recorded statement by J. Francis Fisher regarding the discovery of Morse:

> In the fall of the year 1832 I returned from Europe as a passenger with Mr. Morse in the ship Sully, Captain Pell master. During the voyage the subject of an electric telegraph was one of frequent conversation. Mr. Morse was most constant in pursuing it, and alone the one who seemed disposed to reduce it to a practical test,

---

[9] Morse, *Letters and Journals*, vol. 1, 290.

[10] Samuel Finley Breese Morse, *Samuel F. B. Morse, His Letters and Journals*, vol. 2, ed. Edward Lind Morse (Boston: Houghton Mifflin Company, 1914).

> and I recollect that, for this purpose, he devised
> a system of signs for letters to be indicated and
> marked by a quick succession of strokes or shocks
> of the galvanic current, and I am sure of the fact
> that it was deemed by Mr. Morse perfectly com-
> petent to effect the result stated.[11]

Here is a summary of Samuel Morse's letters, thoughts, and conversations after the initial idea of invention, written by Edward Lind Morse:

> Morse was completely possessed by this new
> idea. He worked over it that day and far into the
> night. His vivid imagination leaped into the fu-
> ture, brushing aside all obstacles, and he realized
> that here in his hands was an instrument capable
> of working inconceivable good. He recalled the
> days and weeks of anxiety when he was hungry
> for news of his loved ones; he foresaw that in
> affairs of state and of commerce rapid commu-
> nication might mean the avoidance of war or the
> saving of a fortune; that, in affairs nearer to the
> heart of the people, it might bring a husband to
> the bedside of a dying wife, or save the life of a
> beloved child; apprehend the fleeing criminal, or
> commute the sentence of an innocent man. His
> great ambition had always been to work some
> good for his fellow men, and here was a means
> of bestowing upon them an inestimable boon.[12]

Here is a statement made by Richard Morse, brother of Samuel Morse, upon meeting him following the initial discovery of the telegraph:

---

[11] Morse, *Letters and Journals*, vol. 2, 11.
[12] Morse, *Letters and Journals*, vol. 2, 13.

> Hardly had the usual greetings passed between us three brothers, and while on our way to my house, before he informed us that he had made, during his voyage, an important invention, which had occupied almost all his attention on shipboard—one that would astonish the world and of the success of which he was perfectly sanguine; that this invention was a means of communicating intelligence by electricity, so that a message could be written down in a permanent manner by characters at a distance from the writer. He took from his pocket and showed from his sketch-book, in which he had drawn them, the kind of characters he proposed to use. These characters were dots and spaces representing the ten digits or numerals, and in the book were sketched other parts of his electro-magnetic machinery and apparatus, actually drawn out in his sketch-book.[13]

Samuel Morse faced the same challenge of communication over distances as everyone else, but he approached the problem differently. He did not work against the blob. He worked against a frame, a frame of his own creation. Morse saw past Figure 1, and through diligence, hard work, discipline, a steady hand, and drawing upon cumulative experience, he created a Figure 2 frame.

He could have been just another bloke accepting the difficulties of the day. That's what everyone around him did. History is glad

---

[13]   Morse, *Letters and Journals*, vol. 2, 17; "Drawings from the Sketchbook of Samuel F. B. Morse," HistoryNet, accessed February 8, 2024, https://www.historynet.com/morses-partner-argued-he-invented-famous-code-to-no-a-vail/drawings-from-the-sketchbook-of-samuel-f-b-morse-illustrating-his-first-conception-of-the-telegraph-drawings-feature-morse-code-rolls-of-paper-tape-to-record-coded-messages-electromagnets/.

he did not. Our world is a different and better place because of Samuel F. B. Morse.

Marriage vs. Divorce, Stability vs. Family Breakdown

The stats are concerning, troubling—you might even say terrifying. For a new marriage, the chances of it ending in divorce over the course of a lifetime are about 42%–45%, pushing up to near 50% if you include separation.[14] That's right, Working Man, it's awfully close to a coin toss. I guess you can call it good news that the annual divorce rate has trended down since 1980 (Appendix, Figure 12),[15] but that is hardly encouraging. Think of the cumulative effect, what this means over the course of four or five generations and beyond. That's a big reason why these days

---

[14] Paul R. Amato, "Interpreting Divorce Rates, Marriage Rates, and Data on the Percentage of Children with Single Parents," National Healthy Marriage Resource Center, accessed March 1, 2024, https://www.healthymarriageinfo.org/wp-content/uploads/2017/12/Interpreting-Divorce-Rat.pdf;
Scott Stanley, "What Is the Divorce Rate, Anyway? Around 42%, One Scholar Believes," Institute for Family Studies, January 23, 2015, https://ifstudies.org/blog/what-is-the-divorce-rate-anyway-around-42-percent-one-scholar-believes/;
Bethany L. Van Vleet and Denise Ann Bodman, "Divorce Rates, Measurement of," in *The Wiley Blackwell Encyclopedia of Family Studies*, ed. Constance L. Shehan, 1st ed., vol. 2 (Hoboken, NJ: John Wiley & Sons, Inc., 2016), 570–573;
Sheela Kennedy and Steven Ruggles, "Breaking Up Is Hard to Count: The Rise of Divorce in the United States, 1980–2010," *Demography* 51, no. 2 (2014): 587–598, https://doi.org/10.1007/s13524-013-0270-9;
W. Bradford Wilcox, "The Evolution of Divorce," *National Affairs*, Fall 2009, https://www.nationalaffairs.com/publications/detail/the-evolution-of-divorce;
Robert Schoen and Nicola Standish, "The Retrenchment of Marriage: Results from Marital Status Life Tables for the United States, 1995," *Population and Development Review* 27, no. 3 (2001): 553–563, https://doi.org/10.1111/j.1728-4457.2001.00553.x;
Robert Schoen and Vladimir Canudas-Romo, "Timing Effects on Divorce: 20th Century Experience in the United States," *Journal of Marriage and Family* 68, no. 3 (2006): 749–758, https://doi.org/10.1111/j.1741-3737.2006.00287.x;
Rune Zahl-Olsen, Frode Thuen, and Birgitte Espehaug, "Divorce and Remarriage in Norway: A Prospective Cohort Study Between 1981 and 2013," *Journal of Divorce and Remarriage* 60, no. 8 (2019): 600–611, https://doi.org/10.1080/10502556.2019.1619378.

[15] W. Bradford Wilcox, ed., *The State of Our Unions: Marriage in America 2009* (University of Virginia: The National Marriage Project, 2009), 75.

you don't see all that many marriages celebrating 40th, 50th, 75th wedding anniversaries.

Married folks just don't stay that way, as they used to. And the children of those broken marriages are bearing the cost. And we call ourselves civilized. Have we no shame?

Longevity in marriage is a Figure 1 problem, a blob. Lots of people never figure it out. The benefits of marriage are crystal clear, yet folks still find it hard to solve, hard to master. In a choice between being the regular chap stumbling through life and failing at key things or being a problem-solver, I choose to solve the problem. How about you, Working Man? What will you do?

Let's apply Chapter 1 principles of problem-solving to this most critical of areas. The benefits of lifelong marriage are immense and carry over generation to generation.[16] It's not out of style to want what is best for your children and grandchildren. If you care about that, what is best for the kiddos, and wish to burnish your own life as well, then let's solve the problem.

Think about your legacy. Think about what you leave behind. What do you want it to say? What tale will be told? Working Man, I challenge you directly. Build a legacy worth leaving. If you accept the challenge, family stability will be at the front of your mind. Do it for the kids, for the people around you. And you personally will be better off for your effort as well.

---

[16] Bridget Mahar, "The Benefits of Marriage," Family Research Council, accessed March 1, 2024, https://downloads.frc.org/EF/EF11B13.pdf;
Robert G. Wood, Sarah Avellar, and Brian Goesling, *The Effects of Marriage on Health: A Synthesis of Recent Research Evidence* (Nova Science Publishers Inc., 2009); Cherese Wiley, "Surprising Health Benefits of Marriage," *Scrubbing In* (blog), Baylor Scott & White Health, November 7, 2016, https://www.bswhealth.com/blog/surprising-health-benefits-marriage;
Brienna Perelli-Harris et al., "Do Marriage and Cohabitation Provide Benefits to Health in Mid-Life?" *Population Research and Policy Review* 37, no. 5 (2018): 703–28, https://doi.org/10.1007/s11113-018-9467-3.

Now, let's break this Figure 1 problem down. We need to break it into components, frame it, and make it a Figure 2 problem. At first glance, and looking at common experience around us, it appears unsolvable. Not so. Here's how.

First, recognize what kind of problem this represents and look for a frame to match it. The problem in the Morse telegraph example is a technical problem and, therefore, required a technical frame. Samuel Morse recognized this up front and so had a chance to succeed.

The plan and desire to achieve family stability, what kind of problem is that? It's a tough one, so we need to get the category right at the start. See it for what it is: a moral problem, requiring a moral frame.

Family stability (i.e., the avoidance of family breakdown), at its heart, is steeped in human behavior driven by choices, by what you value. That is a moral issue. You must see that clearly. All other factors (financial, cultural, social, circumstantial) will take a back seat to the moral choices that will and must be made.

Working Man, take a look back at the subsection above, "The Power of Principles." If you face a problem that is inherently moral in nature, what do you need? You need a foundation, a bedrock, a reference point, a North Star.

You need something bigger than yourself, something that is beyond you. You need a guide that extends further than your own mind. You need themes that stretch back into history and forward into eternity, things that don't end. If you only have yourself, your own impulse, desires, urges, and reactions, you will fail. And the woman next to you, and the children looking up at you, will suffer the cost. Your legacy will carry the consequence of family breakdown. That cost can carry far and wide. Put your heart and soul into this one, Working Man.

Let's prove this point—the need for a foundation deeper than you—by pressing further into a frame. Stats and surveys are helpful here. The causes of divorce are studied with frequency these days, and right at the top of most any list you will find money and sex, sex meaning infidelity.[17] The usual suspects, you might say. Problems surrounding money and sex are issues every couple will face, and failure, divorce, is often tied to these.

Following our principles of problem-solving, let's break things down into components, then frame and solve them one at a time. Remember, problems are solvable if you do not allow them to conglomerate, to bunch together.

Take stock so far. We categorize family stability as a moral problem, requiring a moral frame. We then break this into components, focusing on root causes of divorce. Money and infidelity are two of the biggest. Let's choose one and leave others for later. You will have a lifetime to work on this—they will all come around eventually.

What the heck, let's get personal. Let's choose sex, infidelity, or, stated in the positive sense, remaining faithful. That's right, Working Man, we will discuss the male sex drive.

It's also a practical choice. If the man is faithful in marriage, the chance of solving all other problems goes way up. You now have a base of commitment to work from. Without sexual fidelity, your foundation is fractured. It won't stand up to hard times. Strain will end you.

---

[17] Suany A. Canales, "Common Reasons for Divorce," The Open Repository @ Binghampton (Winter 2021), https://orb.binghamton.edu/cgi/viewcontent.cgi?article=1020&context=hdev_fac;
Shelby B. Scott et al., "Reasons for Divorce and Recollections of Premarital Intervention: Implications for Improving Relationship Education," *Couple Family Psychology* 2, no. 2 (2013): 131–145, https://doi.org/10.1037/a0032025;
Paul R. Amato and Stacey J. Rogers, "A Longitudinal Study of Marital Problems and Subsequent Divorce," *Journal of Marriage and the Family* 59, no. 3 (August 1997): 612–624, https://doi.org/10.2307/353949.

Any frame that is useful at all, that has any chance of success, must be realistic and honest. So, we start by taking the male sex drive as a given, no Puritan sugarcoating allowed. It is raw, relentless, uncompromising, and always seeking fulfillment. It is not that particular about the specific companion involved. Pretty much any female that is of age, not of blood relation, and willing will work just fine. Most won't risk prison over a rendezvous, but most everything else is fair game. The body the Working Man lives in is not very discriminating. Sexual satisfaction is demanded and will be found in some fashion.

Now, back to our proposition above, you need a moral compass, something beyond yourself. Here is your evidence, proof, if you consider it carefully. Follow the logic. If you have only yourself as a reference point, you have only yourself to rely upon. You are bound to the passions, urges, desires, and impulses that create the problem to begin with. Men are not unfaithful because it has proven over time to be a good idea. The consequences and causes of divorce, driven often by infidelity, are established beyond doubt, and they are not positive.

Men are unfaithful because their inherent passion leads them to it. If your North Star is you, you will come right back to yourself. If your bedrock, your foundation, is you, then all your weaknesses and failings are built in. If your reference point is you, then you are all you have.

Good luck. It's hard to solve a problem by depending on you when you are the problem. I would call this impossible, but the hardheaded Working Man can be awfully optimistic, devoid of success, and act contrary to all evidence. Go ahead. Try it again. When you get tired of failure, come back and we can talk.

Working Man, you are inherently a sexual being, fidelity not inherently included, and yet that Working Woman at your side needs faithfulness. She needs to know that she can depend on you. Solving all other problems that a marriage will face demands it.

Back to your North Star, your guidepost, your reference point. What is it? What do you choose? I hope you see that we are at an impasse. If you choose only yourself as a guide, you will do whatever you can get away with. Family stability, then, is not likely. The Working Woman whom you are enraptured with, the one who captured your interest, she cannot rely on you. Your marriage will break down.

I can state clearly for you the guidepost that I have chosen, the North Star, the moral compass, the reference point. I choose the Almighty, the Creator of the Universe, the God of the Hebrews, the One who knits us together in the womb, the Eternal God of the Holy Bible.

Any moral problem requires a moral framework. I have found this moral frame to be reliable and trustworthy. It works. This foundation is solid, a bedrock you can build on.

On with the example. To summarize at present, we face the problem of marriage stability. We categorize this as a moral problem, and we choose a moral frame. In our case, we choose the Holy Bible to provide moral guidance. We take the components one at a time, starting with the male sex drive, then adding the component of fidelity to the raw, natural equation of male sexual drive and satisfaction.

We've reduced the problem to separable components, and we've chosen one as a priority. Now, let's create the frame. Let the moral guide, the Holy Bible, speak on its own clear terms. Let God speak for Himself. Here is what He has to say.

> For this reason a man shall leave his father and
> his mother, and be joined to his wife; and they
> shall become one flesh.
>
> Genesis 2:24

Some Pharisees came to Jesus, testing Him and asking, "Is it lawful for a man to divorce his wife for any reason at all?" And He answered and said, "Have you not read that He who created them from the beginning made them male and female, and said, 'For this reason a man shall leave his father and mother and be joined to his wife, and the two shall become one flesh'? So they are no longer two, but one flesh. Therefore, what God has joined together, no person is to separate."

Matthew 19:3–6

You shall not commit adultery.

Exodus 20:14

Marriage is to be held in honor among all, and the marriage bed is to be undefiled; for God will judge the sexually immoral and adulterers.

Hebrews 13:4

For this is the will of God, your sanctification; that is, that you abstain from sexual immorality; that each of you know how to possess his own vessel in sanctification and honor.

1 Thessalonians 4:3–4

Husbands, love your wives, just as Christ also loved the church and gave Himself up for her.

Ephesians 5:25

That's about as clear as it gets. We have our frame. God loves marriage, He hates adultery, and He commands fidelity. And He will judge mankind accordingly. The Working Man is to get his sexual satisfaction from a lifelong relationship with the Working Woman who will have him.

You might recognize the quote from Exodus 20. That is the Ten Commandments. It is very interesting to study verse 14 in the original Hebrew. Just two words, essentially saying, "No adultery."[18] The Almighty does not mince words. He gets right to the point.

The problem of marriage stability is now a Figure 2 problem, at least this component of it. It is now manageable, something we can solve. Work against the frame, not the blob.

"Hold on a stinkin' minute," says the observant Working Man. We will call him Astute Working Man. Astute Working Man says, "That's all well and fine. You have your frame, a fine one, all fancy and such; Divine commands, all spiritual and approved. Very authoritative. But those sexual desires you describe are still there. They will trample all over your frame and take you right back where you started. The frame doesn't take away the desire. Even if you know the right thing to do, it doesn't mean you will do it."

That's a little rough, Astute Working Man, maybe irreverent but well stated. You are correct. The desires remain and don't necessarily, and absolutely don't automatically, conform to the frame.

We have here the ancient Aristotelian problem, the ancient Plato/Socrates versus Aristotle debate. The idea of the good is important (Plato), but the doing of the good is what matters (Aristotle).[19] Ideas versus action. Actions are what matter.

---

18   Jay P. Green, *The Interlinear Bible—Hebrew, Greek, English* (Peabody MA: Hendrickson Publishers, 1986).

19   *Stanford Encyclopedia of Philosophy* online, s.v., "Aristotle's Ethics," July 2, 2022, https://plato.stanford.edu/entries/aristotle-ethics/.

In truth, it is no debate at all. The idea of the good is critical, and we must have it. It starts with a thought, an idea. We must then act upon this idea for the desired result. Ideas and actions, they must come together.

Back to Astute Working Man's objection to our frame. What if you don't do it? Then the frame is useless. This observation is accurate. And my reply is "Hold that thought." The mechanics, the administration, the working out of the frame for a moral problem have not yet been discussed. We will save that for a later point in our conversation. You first set the frame, and once set, you must take action. Action that recognizes the desires in play. We need to cover a few more concepts, Working Man, and then we will return to this most important question at the end of Chapter 4.

I must also note here that we have covered just one narrow aspect of marriage stability in this example. We will discuss marriage far more broadly in later chapters. There is much more to come, Working Man.

CONCLUSIONS

Problems are coming your way. You can't stop them or change that. To think otherwise is self-delusion. You don't have the ability or purview to stop problems from finding you. Your key choice is in how you respond. Will you whine, cry, rationalize, quit, blame, and otherwise be a pathetic human being, or will you engage and make the world a better place, no matter what life brings your way? That is the decision you must make.

Do something. Do something positive. Face issues head on and make things better. Use the tools and abilities that God has given us. These are acts of faith. Stop trying to control the world around you. It isn't ours to control. We control only one thing: our choice in the moment. We will expound upon this principle later in the "Mental Habits" section.

Live a life of faith by means of a critically important principle: humility. To think, or even attempt to believe, that one is exempt from the stream of problems in this present life can be described in simple terms: arrogant, self-centered, and, most directly put, unbelieving. If I do that, I'm really declaring that God is in control only if I am in control. I am treating the two concepts as one and the same: God is sovereign only if I am sovereign. An attitude and act of faith is to consciously realize and declare that only the first is necessary, not the second.

I hope you can see it, Working Man. The tension between hope and trouble, a tension that drives many to distraction, to rebellion, to frustration, and to poor character has been resolved. It is resolved by your choice to be a problem-solver, by the courage and insight to face every problem and take it from Figure 1 to Figure 2.

Here's a hard and clear fact—problems are a gift. They make you better. Confess, Working Man, we don't learn all that much when things are going well or to our liking. We think it is all because of us. Trouble makes you think, makes you consider—it provides the opportunity to go beyond yourself.

A proper and effective approach to problem-solving falls to Chapter 1 in this book for a reason. This is a dividing-line issue. It separates men from boys, wheat from chaff, serious people from losers and pretenders, and achievers from slackers. The attitude toward problems in life is an internal matter, a matter of the heart and mind, but the choice you make shows up on the outside.

The first outward evidence that you have the right approach is humility. With humility, you get over yourself and get serious about life. People can now depend on you. Working Man, hear me, the Working Woman whom you care about and want to share your life with, she will think the world of you if you excel at this Chapter 1 approach.

The longer-term effect of approaching problems correctly, the evidence that you have it right, is that you now care about the deeper things in life. Themes, tested ideas, foundational principles, and bedrock—these are the things you care about when you face the facts about a problem-filled life. Do you think you are too good to be hassled? Do you consider it beneath you? That you should really be above it all? Working Man, do you blame others? If so, you are a child, not fit for adult life.

Chapter 2

MATTERS OF FAITH

GOD AND CHARACTER: A MATTER FOR CHOOSING

WORKING MAN, THERE are big issues in life that will radically change your daily routine, and with it, your outcome. Next up, we take on a handful of these. We now have a problem-solving approach that I know works. It is tested and tried, proven. Let's use it on the big ideas that will shape your life.

First up, the biggest question of all. Does God exist? Does it matter one way or another? Should you even care? Here we go, Working Man. Let's jump right in.

Let me disclose a little more background. I was raised in a Christian home. My parents brought me up that way and I accepted and adopted those values for myself over the course of time and adulthood. Melissa has a similar background, and we have built our home around this same faith.

We have a deep reverence for all faiths and a respect for anyone with deep conviction. Along with that, we will advocate passionately for Christian belief and practice. We have seen the effect in our lives. It is amazing.

The faith that God gives us, that He calls us to, is not fragile. It is not tenuous or frail. It is not subject to recall. It is not seasonal. It is a faith for all times, all peoples, all cultures, all places, every circumstance, and all conditions. It is a faith for the ages. It is eternal—"Rock of Ages, cleft for me."[20]

But how did Melissa and I come to this faith and make it our own? Was it simple conditioning mandated by our parents? Not in the least. They taught us, no question about that, but that teaching would never survive on its own against the testing that life brings. There must be reasons behind the belief, or it will never last. Life will make sure of that. The reasoning must stand up under pressure.

I'm going to talk you through the reasoning, our experience. You will see in this conversation another example of how to frame and break problems into components. We'll apply the Chapter 1 problem-solving technique to this biggest of issues in life: What about God? Should you spend any time on the topic, or is it just a waste? Does it add any value? I will relate this to you just as we have lived it. It is the largest of Figure 1 problems taken to a Figure 2 frame, step by step. Hold on to your seat; on we go.

After Oklahoma State University, as Melissa and I settled into our banking career, I had a very interesting and influential

---

[20] Augustus Montague Toplady, "Rock of Ages," *Congregational Church Music with 150 Psalms and Hymns* (New Haven, CT: Durrie & Peck, 1854), http://openhymnal.org/Lyrics/Rock_of_Ages-Toplady.html.

experience—one of those life-shaping experiences. I treasure it to this day.

Remember our background—raised in a farming/ranching community in rural Texas and New Mexico. Faith is taken for granted there, widely practiced and firmly believed. Old-fashioned America is everywhere. Someone stepping out of 1776 America into our community would not feel out of place. Once acclimated to modern tech, they would fit right in.

In the banking world, I found myself working with a lot of atheists. I'm not sure why that was the case, but the atheist view was easy to find in the finance industry. I can easily remember 30 or more colleagues who were adamantly of the atheist persuasion.

There were three in particular whom I was pretty close with. We were on project teams together and traveled together internationally. Many of you know the scene: long hours, intense work, lots of pressure to perform, late-night restaurant meals, long meetings in the conference room, and follow-up. This phase covered a period of about seven years, two major companies, and several continents.

In our faith, as with many adherents, you learn a lot about sharing your beliefs, how to open conversation, how to make folks comfortable, how to treat them with respect, etc. But with this crew, those three, none of that was necessary. They made sure the topic came up. They were very aggressive and inquisitive. They brought it up every chance we had. What about this idea? Why do you think this? How could you possibly believe that? And on and on it went.

I found it exhausting, exhilarating, fascinating, amazingly interesting—a whole range of emotions and responses were involved. Above all, to me, it was formative, a real education. I found myself reading, studying, considering, and preparing for our next exchange. I knew it would come. I wanted to be prepared.

Above all, I wanted to be correct, to be sound in my thinking. If these dudes could poke holes in my reasoning, that had to be considered. What if I was wrong and they were right? I felt a need to take that seriously. To this day, I am appreciative of that experience.

The first thing that struck me out of these conversations is that it isn't primarily the scientific argument that drives the atheistic view. That was not at the core of their objection. They certainly raised scientific points about the world, how it works, and how it began. But these atheists, the everyday kind, as opposed to the atheist trying to sell books or making TV appearances, understood that science can never truly settle the issue.

Science resides inside the universe. It is a tool. We use it to explore and understand the world around us. Science is bound to, dwells entirely within, and is a product of the universe. Science is not a cause—it is a tool to discover and observe.

The question of God's existence and first cause rest outside the universe and therefore outside of science. Science gives evidence, but there will never be a scientific test that proves or disproves the existence of God.

A serious atheist, like the three I came to know so well, understands this. Evidence is laid bare, presented for all to see, and people must consider and choose. The question stands before us, and we must decide.

A Universe by Design

I will scream from the rooftops that God exists and that this universe is His by design. My choice is made, and I will live it out. Why would I make that choice? Consider a few things.

Behold the physical fact and entity of the universe. Where did it come from? Break the question down to its most basic elements;

strip all else away. You only have two choices, only two possible replies. Either the universe is by design, and therefore there is a Designer, or it is a blind, random accident. Cause or happenstance—that is your choice set.

Don't get fooled by high words or sophistry. "The universe has always been." That's a favorite of the agnostic/atheistic crowd. Oh? And how so? The question still stands. How did it get here? The question is as stubborn as the universe itself. It will not go away.

Answer it. Blind chance or design? I will readily admit the possibility that all we see and enjoy just happened to pop up, but I also have to say that if the universe is an accident, it is one heck of an accident. My goodness, what an outcome, all by chance. I don't think so. Consider a bit more; think of the "accidents" that had to occur, at the beginning and all the way through to now.

Ponder the cell of any organism. Take a swab, gather some cell tissue, make it easy and painless, and place it under a microscope. What do you see? Roughly, from the mid-19th century through the first half of the 20th century, the scientific assumption held that at the bottom of organic life, held in each cell, was some sort of basic plasma or gel composed of uncomplicated building block chemicals. Nothing special, something that could spontaneously form under the right conditions.

Spontaneous generation, as it was called, was the working scientific theory for many years. A chief proponent of this widely accepted idea was Ernst Haeckel.[21] Haeckel famously said the cell is nothing more than "a simple little lump of albuminous combination of carbon."[22]

---

21 Gloria Robinson, "Ernst Heinrich," *Encyclopedia Britannica*, last modified February 12, 2024, https://www.britannica.com/biography/Ernst-Haeckel.

22 John Farley, *The Spontaneous Generation Controversy from Descartes to Oparin* (Baltimore, MD: Johns Hopkins University Press, 1977).

Then something happened through the course of the 20th century, something amazing. Along came the electron microscope.[23] This new technology allowed detailed examination of tiny things, like what happens inside a cell. What it revealed was astounding and revolutionary to biology—complexity, beyond anything imaginable. Inside a cell is like a factory with complex processes, precise signals, flows and routing of materials, including many interdependencies.

There was nothing simple or basic about any of it. Much of it can be described as "irreducible complexity."[24] If you remove a single component, the entire system fails. In other words, laying out a proto-path where blind, random chance over extended periods of time could result in the observed process inside a cell would be impossible. So much for the blind, random universe.

And that is a fair summary of science, where it stands today and all that it has taught us—complexity. Step out on a clear, dark night and observe the sky. The wonder you see does not end there. It extends in every direction, down to the smallest electron and subatomic particle, up to the farthest galaxy, to every corner and crevice of this planet and all else that we see or have yet to discover. Pick a field of science: physics, biology, medicine, astrophysics—you name it. I dare you to look at it honestly and call it simple. Not so. You find complexity everywhere you turn.

So, I say again, the universe may very well be a random accident, but, oh my goodness, what an incredible, amazing accident it is. I don't think so. Let's listen to the apostle Paul and take in his view.

---

[23] Detlev H. Kruger, Peter Schneck, and Hans R. Gelderblom, "Helmut Ruska and the Visualisation of Viruses," *The Lancet* 355, no. 9216 (2000): 1713–1717, https://doi.org/10.1016/s0140-6736(00)02250-9;
Barry R. Masters, *History of the Electron Microscope in Cell Biology* (Hoboken, NJ: John Wiley and Sons, Ltd, 2009).

[24] Michael Behe, *Darwin's Black Box: The Biochemical Challenge to Evolution* (New York: Simon & Schuster, 1996, 2006).

> For since the creation of the world God's invisible attributes, that is, His eternal power and divine nature, have been clearly perceived, being understood by what has been made.
>
> Romans 1:20

The universe stands as an eternal testimony to … something. What? Blind chance or design. You choose. I've made my choice—design, therefore a Designer.

After the examination of the physical complexity and wonder of this world, which is something to behold, you have another fact to consider, which is every bit as formidable—the implications. In a blind, random universe, there is no hope, no meaning, no purpose whatsoever. Do not step around this fact. Face it in full. You are not a person with purpose. You are an accident—a big, fat nothing.

The implications of the choice above, blind chance or design, are not trivial. Consider the facts. If a blind, random universe holds no purpose, no hope, no meaning, then why are these the things that really drive us? How could a blind universe by chance create the intangible things of life, the things we really cling to?

What does the human heart really rest on? Love, hope, goodness, sacrifice, honor, devotion, nobility, courage, altruism, valor—these things drive us. These things make us whole. We live for the intangibles. A blind universe could never create this. It is an impossibility.

We hug a spouse in the quiet of the morning, not because of the latest insight of astrophysics but because our heart is filled with love and comfort. A blind universe has no capability, no insight, no prior knowledge, and no prior incentive to produce this. In that world—blind, cold, random—there is only the goal of survival and the power to achieve it. Nothing else.

At the core of our being, deep in our soul, rests the need for purpose. We need life to matter. This is an intangible that, when embraced and held high, produces tangible results with amazing benefits for all to see. Why are we made this way? Did a blind, random universe produce this? I say, "No way."

These factors, the intangibles, require a preexisting intelligence to bring them into existence. They are not random. The notion of irreducible complexity, noted above, is a formidable and binding concept when looking at the physical and biological universe. Consider the same idea as applied to the intangible items. What aspects of faith, love, hope, courage, etc. could be created except by someone who had full knowledge of these concepts prior to their existence? Blind chance? No. A normal person, of normal honesty, calls this design.

Working Man, wake up. The human heart, the human spirit, is no accident and neither is the world around us. Reach out and touch the Divine. Connect to something bigger than this world and bigger than you. Faith is the avenue. I challenge you: Make up your mind. Take the step. It is the best way to live.

The Question of Character

My atheist friends were very forceful and open, and we had deep, hours-long conversations. As stated above, because they were both intelligent and honest, they did not rest their main argument against the Divine on the scientific. They knew the final score on that. So, what made them answer in the negative when facing the question of the Almighty?

Through all our conversations, I realized that what really raised an obstacle they could not clear was the issue over character, God's character and nature as understood by simple observation. They look at the hard things in life, they look at children's suffering, they look at what people do to each other and say, "Could a loving God let that go on?" That's what really trips them up. It makes them a firm "no" on faith.

Take a visit to the nearest hospital. You will see it up close and personal. We have all experienced it in some fashion. Melissa and I had an especially poignant encounter in one of the suburbs we called home. Neighbors down the street had kids about the age of ours. Melissa and the neighbor mom became close friends.

One day their three-year-old was complaining of stomach pains, so her mom took her to the doctor. What they discovered was terrifying to any parent. Cancer had wrapped around every major organ and filled her body cavity. The chance of survival was low. This was a normal three-year-old little girl, as cute as she could be, now with a shattered world discovered in a single visit to the doctor.

Everyone can imagine and comprehend the pain, horror, expense, and hardship this three-year-old and her family went through, for a long time. Their journey was horrific. Fortunately, the treatments worked, and the young child survived and prospers to this day. But this might not have been the outcome—cancer, this cancer in particular, often overcomes.

To bring the atheist's view into focus, imagine a particular scene in the scenario above. Suppose I was standing next to this family, and I had the cure for the cancer in a vial in my pocket. And I refused to hand it over. What would you think of me? What would happen to me?

I will state it plainly, capturing clearly what my atheist friends thought. If I did what God does, as is commonly on display, you would not worship me and consider me Divine. You would not consider me to have "higher wisdom." You would regard me as a psychotic sociopath. You would think me a criminal, not fit for open society. You would arrest me and throw me in prison.

And there you have it, Working Man. The strongest, most cogent argument available for the atheist view. God may exist, He may not, we may never know, but look at what He does. You cannot trust Him. He stands there and watches while the world suffers and burns. Innocent people—kids—suffer and He does nothing. I would never get away with that. Why would I put faith in someone Who does?

If you need a literary prompt regarding the depths of despair this life can take you to, I highly recommend the book of Lamentations, or *Night* by Elie Wiesel. Most of you have enough in your personal life to know that life is not easy—the point is beyond debate. Life is fragile, uncertain, full of pain and heartache.

The atheist poses a serious argument. It is intelligent, reasoned, and backed by facts and experience. It is an argument that demands consideration. It deserves such.

Let's consider it. No doubt, life is full of hard things. Unjust things, things nobody would want to endure. We accept that as a fact and ask the follow-on question. Where is God when these things happen? What is His disposition as the crap show of life unfolds? Does He stand aloof, examining coldly our response?

The atheist says, "Yes, He does." But, Working Man, that is not the final word. Take a look.

> Even though I walk through the valley of the shadow of death, I fear no evil; for Thou art with me.
>
> Psalms 23:4

> Because He is at my right hand, I will not be shaken.
>
> Psalms 16:8

> Behold, the virgin shall be with child, and shall bear a Son, and they shall call His name Immanuel, which translated means, God with us.
>
> Matthew 1:23

Ask the question again. Where is God when we suffer, when life is tragic? He is right there with you. He suffers right along with you. He feels everything you feel. He is not cold and aloof. He is right there in the heartache with you. His name is Immanuel, God with us.

"Why would He do that?" you ask. Why would God not change things and take away the injustice and the suffering and make everything right? If I had that kind of power, that is what I would do.

Well, Working Man, there is a lot about this world that we don't understand and never will, but there is part of this conundrum that we can answer. We can know the things that we really need to know.

The answer is twofold, one part instructive and one part encouraging and inspirational. The instructive part says this, stated clearly by the apostle Peter.

> But by His word the present heavens and earth are being reserved for fire, kept for the day of judgment and destruction of ungodly people. But do not let this one fact escape your notice, beloved, that with the Lord one day is like a thousand years, and a thousand years like one day. The Lord is not slow about His promise, as some count slowness, but is patient toward you, not willing for any to perish, but for all to come to repentance.
>
> 2 Peter 3:7–9

> But according to His promise we are looking for new heavens and a new earth, in which righteousness dwells. Therefore, beloved, since you look for these things, be diligent to be found spotless and blameless by Him, at peace, and regard the patience of our Lord as salvation.
>
> 2 Peter 3: 13–15

We all desire for the world to be right—no harm, no injustice, no suffering. The atheist and secular hope for this as well. And God has promised just that, a new day.

Consider a moment, Working Man. When righteousness comes, what becomes of unrighteousness? When the perfect comes, what of the imperfect? When the perfect comes, the imperfect cannot abide. When purity descends, the impure cannot remain.

When we ask for the world to be made right, we are really asking for judgment. We are asking God to wipe out the impure and for righteousness to reign. And He will do exactly that but only in His time, by His purpose, by His own hand.

The instructive part of our answer is this—while this deeply flawed world rolls on, the window of grace and choice remains open. God stands with open arms, calling us to walk in His Grace. Regard the patience of our Lord as salvation. The gates of Heaven welcome all, calling you to enter.

There will be a day when choice is no longer open; choices will have been made—past tense. That day belongs to the Almighty. It is beyond our reach. The timing and circumstance are His alone. In the meantime, regardless of difficulty and trial, live with joy and a clear mind. Live with a heart full of faith, hope, and love. Your testimony, your witness, will bring others in, pointing the way. May it be as many as possible.

And there is more, Working Man. There is inspiration. There is vast encouragement as you tread this difficult life with a heart of faith fixed on the God of hope and love. Consider His Son, Christ the Messiah.

Christ lived the only perfect life this world has ever seen. He wronged no one. He elevated humanity as never seen prior. He lived out Divine Nature in a wicked, twisted world for all to see. And He was murdered for it, executed in cold blood.

And then He rose again. The tomb is empty. God raised Him from the dead for all at the time to see. By overwhelming personal witness, Christ lived, was crucified, and rose again, leaving the tomb and conversing with several hundred witnesses over many days.

He then left His followers with instructions on advancing His kingdom and living the life of a disciple of Christ. There is something very important to note in this progression of events, something deeply encouraging and inspiring.

Christ lived a perfect life, but what kind of world did He leave behind? What of Roman rule? Did He end that? What of religious, political, and social corruption? Did that cease with His appearance? What of His followers? Were they of impeccable quality? Did they live flawless lives?

Hardly. None of that happened. Was the world wiped clean with Divine antiseptic? Was everything made right, with all injustice ended? You know the answer. No, it wasn't.

So what do we make of that? What do we conclude by observing that Christ left behind a very flawed world? I won't pretend or attempt to be comprehensive, but there is one thing I know, one thing that fills me with courage, hope, passion, and purpose.

Christ is not fixated on perfection. He has not called us to perfection but to faithfulness. Perfection is not something that I can do, and He knows that. Faithfulness, however, I can do.

I should live life with courage, with hope, with passion, with purpose and fix my vision on faithfulness. No matter what, I will get up and try again. God has not called me to something that I cannot do. Perfection is not my purview, not my problem. I am called to what I can do—remain faithful. I am capable of that.

Working Man, you will be faithful to your wife, and someone down the street will cheat on theirs. Be faithful anyway. You will be honest, and someone near you will lie. Tell the truth anyway. You will work hard. Some welfare brat will steal from the public, including you. Work hard anyway. Because all comes to judgment in that final day. God will have the final say.

One of the most powerful missives you can read is "The Final Analysis" by Mother Teresa.[25] I bow to her words of wisdom. Read them and be instructed.

The broad instruction and deep encouragement should be clear to see. I hope you find it useful, just as I have. The toughest argument against faith, the belief of the atheist that warrants serious response, when considered, actually turns to points of instruction and great inspiration.

Working Man, remember, a world without faith, without God, is a world without hope. A world without hope soon becomes a world without love. We need all three. The human heart demands it, even as we refuse to acknowledge it.

---

[25] Mother Teresa, "The Final Analysis," accessed February 11, 2024, http://www.wow-zone.com/final.htm.

Belief = Purpose

I have a proposition for you. I ask you to consider it carefully. The atheist will scoff. The secular will have disdain. But you, Working Man, if you heed my words, you will be a very happy pilgrim through this life, doing all the good you can along the way, heading for a better end.

Here's the proposition: build your life around these intangibles—faith, hope, and love. Make these the core of your existence. Then, upon this basis, secure the tangibles—job, income, material things, and objectives. You will be a much happier person and, consequently, much more productive and fulfilled.

And now for the best part. That Working Woman you can't stop thinking about? The one who steals your thoughts and stirs up that deep-down desire that you try to hide, except when you are with her? She will love you every day for it. She will love you fiercely, passionately, loyally, with no end. You will have pleasure and comfort beyond your highest view.

You will have purpose. Purpose that drives you, fulfills you, and sets your priorities in order. Purpose with no end, no expiration. Purpose that crafts and shapes you into a real man, a Working Man whom a Working Woman refuses to live without. She will want you with a passion and desire that will shake you, that will leave you in awe of what is possible. Your life will truly never be the same.

You see, these intangibles—faith, hope, and love—they are traveling companions. They tend to arrive and depart together. Now, understand, I refer to your experience of them, not their existence. They always abide, without fail they are available, but they don't always affect human nature. That is up to us.

The 20th century has demonstrated beyond dispute what man looks like when he pursues power: wars without end. The 21st century isn't looking much better. We have never been more efficient or effective in killing each other.

Is that the point in life: the power to survive and nothing else? It can be. It depends on what you choose. There is better available. Choose it, live it, and see the result. You will be pleased, and you will be better.

Life with Abundant Purpose: Concluding Thoughts

Working Man, with God there is purpose in abundance, more than you can possibly imagine. Go ahead, explore, and see if you can find a limit to it. I never have. The journey is incredible, fulfillment without end.

Without God, with just yourself, well, all I can say is "Good luck." With only yourself, to say that you have an inadequate reference point, an unsure guidepost, an insecure foundation, is an understatement for all time.

Here is a summary of key points regarding purpose and its role in life:

- Life is about purpose: "What am I trying to achieve?" We should have an objective in front of us, a goal to aim for, or something we are striving to create.

- All honest work is noble and should be viewed as ministry.

- Freedom is the natural desire of mankind because we are driven by the need for purpose. We are made this way.

- Free economies prosper because they are steeped in the principle of service. Individual freedom is harnessed to serve and meet the needs of others. This gives purpose to both individuals and nations. The entire world benefits.

- The freedom and purpose of productivity is the future of mankind, the entire human race. This is the gateway to peace and prosperity, a future worth having.

- The intangibles in life—chiefly faith, hope, and love—should come first. Build your life on these and then secure the tangibles. The heart is made so.

- A life with purpose is a life well lived.

- A life grounded in the intangibles and driven by the purpose to achieve will build a legacy that is noble, honorable, and a sight to behold.

MENTAL HABITS: CHOOSE THE STRUCTURE CAREFULLY

Working Man, let's focus on the mind. We choose our mental habits. Choose carefully—the implications are awesome. You can be a self-centered you-know-what. In that case, good luck with that Working Woman you would like to keep. She won't stand for much of that. If you treat her like property, don't expect her to stay around.

Or you can think bigger than yourself. Placing your faith, and centering your mind, on the Almighty makes a massive difference in everyday life. Of high import, you become the Working Man whom the Working Woman wants to keep around.

If I had to choose a single piece of literature that describes the Western mind, especially the American mind, it would be "Invictus" by William Ernest Henley. Just one verse, actually, "I am the captain of my soul."[26]

---

[26] William Ernest Henley, "Invictus," Poetry Foundation, accessed February 11, 2024, https://www.poetryfoundation.org/poems/51642/invictus.

Okay, that sounds great, but take stock. Grab a pen and paper and make a list. Write down all the things you control. I mean truly control, things you can guarantee. Go ahead. Yea, it's a short list, no?

Admit it. You can't guarantee your next breath, your next heartbeat. The next moment could be your last. So much for being the captain of anything. We don't control much.

Here's another proposition for your consideration, Working Man. I only control one thing, just a single item—my choice in the moment. What I do and say right now is the only thing I can guarantee. Tomorrow, the next minute—these are beyond my grasp.

If you insist on adherence to the *Invictus* premise, then read it with reality in mind. "I am the captain of my soul, right here in this moment. Nothing further."

And, with a belief in the Almighty and purpose driven by Eternity, that's all I need. I can accomplish everything I need to in life with that one point of control.

There are two mental models to study and choose between: one you want and one you don't. Using the lessons of Chapter 1, let's look at this choice and break it down, keeping it simple. The first, the sovereignty model, is the natural state of mankind—the one you shouldn't want. This is the one you will choose without inspiration to do better. It's short sighted, self-centered, and doomed to fail—kind of like human nature.

The Sovereignty Model

- I choose what I prefer and rationalize everything else around it.

- I am "sovereign" in my choices and conduct.

- Decision-making begins with what I prefer versus gathering facts. Facts are deferred, ignored, or discarded based on my preference.

- If I am a believer, I have a limited view of the manner in which God speaks and gives guidance. I center on my own thoughts, heart, and mind. Evidence, facts, consequences, views of others, etc., are given lower weight or little regard.

- I act as though I can control the thoughts, actions, and words of those around me.

- I arrange the views and behaviors of people to suit my preference and "sovereign" choices.

- In excess or extreme, I consider others and their views to be evil if they differ from me. Any offense is a violation of my "sovereignty."

- What offends my preference must be wrong and eliminated.

The second, the stewardship model, stands in contrast. Working Man, I challenge you yet again, take the second model and make it your own. You will have a better life.

The Stewardship Model

- I am given gifts by God's Hand and through His Grace. I am responsible for using and developing those to their highest and best use.

- I am sovereign over one thing and one thing only: my choice in the present moment. I can control nothing else.

- I am keenly aware that I can't guarantee my next breath, let alone outcomes.

- God's sovereignty is complete. His purview is limited by nothing. My sovereignty is highly limited, designed in its proper use to render me a steward, not a sovereign lord.

- I develop over a lifetime a full view of God's method of guidance and leading: Scriptures, His inner voice, the audible voice (rare), dreams (rare), visions (rare), circumstance, events, empirical facts (all truth is from God; facts are by His creative hand), conversation with friends, input from others, etc.

- I have a reverence for facts. I bow my knee to things that are true.

- Facts—what is true—are from God, meant to benefit us all. Satan can never deal in truth, only deception.

- I am a steward, living as a vessel for His Divine purpose, crafted by His creative hand.

Most folks do not engage in true, honest decision-making. They choose up front what they prefer and arrange or ignore facts as necessary to keep that preference. This is better called rationalizing, not decision-making.

True decision-making starts by gathering facts, whatever is true and relevant. Once these facts are carefully and properly considered, preference will be applied at the end of the process, resulting in a decision. Preference is always involved. Humans can decide in no other fashion. However, we choose the order, the process of a choice in the making.

The second mental model, the stewardship model, follows this method. The first mental model, the sovereignty model, is the opposite and leads to rationalizing.

So choose carefully, Working Man. One model will give you a happy, lifelong marriage. One will leave you divorced and lonely.

One will make a Working Woman happy to be at your side. One will leave her nowhere to be found. One leaves a great legacy. The other is empty.

Make a choice and live it out. I've made mine. I think you know what it is.

Chapter 3

MARRIAGE OF A DIFFERENT ORDER

KEEP IT SIMPLE

WE'VE COVERED A lot of ground, some big ideas. I hope you can see the power of the problem-solving technique from Chapter 1. It will truly change your life.

Let's not stop now. Go big or go home. Let's tackle what is probably the second biggest idea you will face—marriage.

The marriage bond is miraculous in form and outcome. As a man and woman unite under the precept of marriage, the union becomes a separate, unique personality. There is no one marriage like another. Each one, over time, forms into a distinct expression of grace. God's plan is worked out through this expression. Each partner rounds out the other, creating a separate unit that is one of a kind. Marriage is sacred, to be held in honor.

Modern culture tears continuously at this bond. Those with memories carrying back to the 1960s can recall the grim sequence of degradation. An early signal of the trouble to come was the disastrous and deeply misguided notion of separating sex and love, embodied in the sexual revolution. Sex could be for pleasure only, no obligations required. We will explore this idea in detail in the next chapter.

Following this grave mistake was the acceptance of teenage promiscuity, marriage infidelity, divorce on demand, abortion on demand, acceptance of single-parent homes, and every variation of family structure imaginable. The statistics covered in the marriage stability example of Chapter 1 tell a dark tale. The cumulative effect over generations is staggering.

The latest cultural movement is fully sanctioned same-sex marriage. Those committed to traditional marriage for moral or religious reasons see this as a sequential step on the road to decline for the family and the bedrock of society. The traditional, biological family unit has taken severe blows the last few decades. Its demise and associated societal consequences are clear at this point.[27]

---

[27] Wendy Manning, Susan Brown, and Bart Stykes, "Same-Sex and Different-Sex Cohabiting Relationship Stability," *Demography* 53, no. 4 (2016): 937–953, https://doi.org/10.1007/s13524-016-0490-x;
Judith Wallerstein, Julia Lewis, and Sandra Blakeslee, *The Unexpected Legacy of Divorce: A 25 Year Landmark Study* (Westport, CT: Hyperion, 2000);
Diane Medved, *The Case Against Divorce* (New York: Donald I. Fine Inc., 1989);
Barbara Dafoe Whitehead, *The Divorce Culture* (New York: Alfred Knopf, 1997);
Shannon Grant, *Divorce: Risk Factors, Patterns and Impact on Children's Well-Being* (Happuage, NY: Nova Science Publishers, 2016);
Libertad Gonzalez and Tarja Viitanen, "The Long-Term Effects of Legalizing Divorce on Children," *Oxford Bulletin of Economics and Statistics* 80, no. 2 (2018): 237–57, https://doi.org/10.1111/obes.12200;
Alison Clarke-Stewart and Cornelia Brentano, "Effects of Divorce on Children," in *Divorce: Causes and Consequences*, (New Haven, CT: Yale University Press, 2006), 106–30, http://www.jstor.org/stable/j.ctt1npfks;
Margaret Harper McCarthy, ed., *Torn Asunder: Children, the Myth of the Good Divorce, and the Recovery of Origins* (Grand Rapids, MI: William B. Eerdmans Publishing Company, 2017).

I realize my words here are controversial, even inflammatory to some, especially the statement on gay marriage. It comes down to bedrock, to foundation: Upon what do you build your life? If you take Scripture as your moral base, your North Star, as I do, then we should state it plainly. There is no such thing as gay marriage. It doesn't exist. God never intended it, and it is nowhere to be found in the Good Book. There is no support for it whatsoever in the Holy Bible.

However, we abide in this secular world, in the here and now. Many do not hold my view of Scripture as our moral guide, and we need to live together. We need a civil arrangement in civic society that we can share in tolerable fashion. As such, I fully recognize that gay marriage, now legally recognized, is not going away. As a secular and civic matter, it is settled. I accept that.

I also hold forth the fact that the world is adrift. The moral base upon which most stand is fractured with significant, negative effect. In light of this, I am bold enough to call us back, back to eternal mores, to things that do not drift or fracture, to things that have always been and will always remain. Those that sense truth in this call will find solace, instruction, wisdom, and great hope in these pages. If you seek those deeper things, Working Man, you have a friend. Let's walk and converse together.

What is a soul to do that cares one whit about traditional family life? Let's return once again to the problem-solving methods of Chapter 1, "Principles of Success." Marriage can be complex. The very notion of blending two individual lives and separate personalities in a pressure-packed, competitive world filled with uncertainty, disappointment, tragedy, and seemingly endless change will bring a load of complexity, to say the least.

We have a Figure 1 problem—a blob that is shape-shifting, opaque, threatening, uncertain. A Figure 1 problem to beat all. Do we dare attempt taking this to a Figure 2 problem? Is it foolish to break it down into components, frame them, and solve them one at a time?

Are there rational persons in existence that would dare say marriage can be reduced to a very few principles, virtually guaranteeing success if they are followed? What person would be so bold as to declare to the world that the immense complexity of creating a thriving marriage in a modern environment can be reduced to a few key ideas?

That would be us, Working Man. We will attempt the feat and summon the boldness. We might not make the daily talk shows doing such things, but that isn't what we care much about, is it? No, we care about daily life. We want things to work out here in everyday land.

If you insist that everything is complex, with no workable solutions, you are intentionally causing everything to become and remain a blob, a Figure 1 problem. That isn't much of a contribution. Life already hands you that. Don't make it worse. Solve a problem. Don't curl up and cry. That's why God gave you abilities; that's why He gave you a brain—use it.

Complexity and conflict sell, no doubt about it. Modern social life is built on it. But if you embrace complexity and the resulting conflict through daily life, as a matter of habit, you will be divorced or single, maybe both. Working Woman isn't looking for someone to fight with. She wants someone to live with. Be a problem-solver, Working Man. You will stand a better chance of being that someone.

First up, straight from the examples of Chapter 1, we need to categorize this challenge. Is it a technical problem like the Morse telegraph example of Chapter 1? No, not really. Many issues within marriage can be technical or medical in nature, but at this point, we are looking at the general nature of marriage and what makes it thrive. As you live out a marriage, specific challenges may fall into a different category. Monthly cash flow problems are an example. These would be technical, or financial, in nature and require a financial frame.

Instead we are starting at ground level, marriage itself, the entity. At the very beginning, or foundational level, of marriage, I say loudly and firmly that it is a moral problem; therefore, it requires a moral frame.

Be careful here, Working Man. It's easy to get tangled up in less important issues, side issues, or lower-priority issues. The wreckage of many a marriage is found on the rocks of side issues. The couple never dug down and got serious about what really matters.

A point to ponder, soberly—whatever you cling to in lieu of what matters will be lost. Whatever you lose in lieu of what matters will be gained. This is God's law, how His universe operates. There is much to consider and discuss on this point, but I will focus on marriage, our topic at hand. We will leave the rest for discussion outside of this book.

Many engage in marriage strictly for utilitarian reasons. They marry because they want to be happy, or they don't want to be lonely, or they just want kids, or they see financial benefit, or that guy or gal is really hot, etc. If you marry because you want to be happy, you won't be happy, and you probably won't stay married.

The problem with circumstantial happiness—utilitarian happiness—is that things change over time. Kids grow up, leave home, and build lives of their own. Physical beauty fades. Annoying habits can stack up over time; money may come and may go. But if you dig deep and understand what makes marriage tick, why and how it is formed, you will marry, you will stay married, and you will find happiness beyond all expectations.

The argument in favor of a moral foundation, a moral frame, for marriage is the same as in the marriage stability example of Chapter 1. The most important elements in a marriage relate to behavior: your actions, your beliefs, the choices you make. Folks will carry on these days about compatibility, shared goals in life, common interests, on and on, endlessly. All of that fades into secondary status. What you believe and how you behave are what really matter.

That, Working Man, is a moral problem requiring a moral frame. The resolution of the foundation of marriage inside a moral framework becomes a firm bedrock upon which you can build a lifelong, stable, family relationship. As mentioned above, many other specific items can come up, requiring a different frame, but you need to start at the very bottom, the foundation. Dig deep. Get this right, and all else can be addressed in due time. If you get the frame wrong at the start, nothing else really matters. You won't even get to most of it. Failure will strike early.

As stated prior, a moral frame requires a base, a bedrock, something bigger than yourself. We worked through that carefully in the second example of Chapter 1 and in Chapter 2. We stick with the same bedrock here in Chapter 3—the Almighty and His Scriptures.

We will use some of the same material as in Chapter 1, but here we are taking a very different perspective. In the prior example of infidelity, we were looking at a specific problem that threatens marriage stability. In this chapter, we are looking at everything that threatens marriage stability, all of it together. When you start a marriage, every threat imaginable is against you. You must have a foundation to match.

That's quite a task. Let's proceed. First, let's list the foundational statements made by the Almighty regarding marriage. Two of these are the same as in Chapter 1, but let's add one more.

And God created man in His own image, in the image of God He created him; male and female He created them. And God blessed them; and God said to them, "Be fruitful and multiply, and fill the earth, and subdue it; and rule over the fish of the sea and over the birds of the sky, and over every living thing that moves on the earth."

Genesis 1:27–28

For this reason a man shall leave his father and his mother, and be joined to his wife; and they shall become one flesh.

Genesis 2:24

Some Pharisees came to Jesus, testing Him and asking, "Is it lawful for a man to divorce his wife for any reason at all?" And He answered and said, "Have you not read that He who created them from the beginning made them male and female, and said, 'For this reason a man shall leave his father and mother and be joined to his wife, and the two shall become one flesh'? So they are no longer two, but one flesh. Therefore, what God has joined together, no person is to separate."

Matthew 19:3–6

Much can be said about the words "subdue" and "rule" in Genesis 1:27–8. For our purposes here, we need only point out one thing. The notion, the idea, is stewardship, making the most of what God has provided. In other words, there is a lot of work to be done.

There is a reason I proposed the stewardship model in Chapter 2. It is the only mental model up to the task. God has given us a stewardship task. A stewardship mindset must therefore be employed.

As stated at the opening of this chapter, marriage belongs to the Almighty. It is His institution, not ours. He gave it to us for specific reasons. Modern culture has done everything imaginable to dilute, weaken, rebrand, decimate, disown, dissolve, redefine, dumb down, and otherwise nullify the institution of marriage, and yet it stands. There is no substitute for the nuclear family, and there never will be.

What does the bumper sticker say? "Thank God for normal families. You wouldn't be here without them."

Here's an eye-opening observation, Working Man. Notice when God chose to create marriage: in the Garden of Eden, before the fall of mankind, before Genesis Chapter 3. That's the only social institution for which that is true in all of the Bible. Think of it. The law of Moses, all civic organizations, all governments, all orders of worship—all of these came after the fall of man and were redemptive in nature.

That's a big deal. Marriage is not God's redemptive plan for mankind; marriage is God's original plan for mankind. Marriage was God's plan for man right from the start.

Don't fight against it, Working Man. You will be fighting against God Himself and all of human history. I can't help you with that, other than to say, "Don't do it." It's not smart. You will be wasting your time, and you will fail.

Work with it. Get in agreement with the One who made marriage to begin with.

Take a hard look at the three passages of Scripture above. Look for themes, foundational ideas that we can build on, bedrock to stand on. Look first at Genesis 1:27–8, the stewardship inferred and commanded. That means a lot of work, and in the fallen world we now inhabit, that means problem-solving—together, husband and wife, as a unit. Okay, store that idea away. We will come back to it.

Now look at Genesis 2:24 and Matthew 19:3–6. Again, look for themes, foundation, or bedrock to stand on. It's hard to look away from that phrase "one flesh." The man and woman shall become one flesh. And God help the one who thinks he can tear it apart. Christ is clear about that in Matthew.

The language is fascinating: "What God has joined together," "shall become one flesh," "be joined to his wife," "no person is to separate," and "they are no longer two, but one." The ideas run deep. The union referenced here, created by God, is not superficial in any sense. It means everything you are, everything you have, and everything you will ever be. Everything you think, dream, plan, or may face in life—all of it joined together, across two humans. Where there stood two people, now stands one entity.

And we are talking about a man and a woman here. A million words could be written about those differences alone—maybe 10 million, a bunch. And then we have two distinct, specific, individual personalities on top of that, plus backgrounds and families—all different. And then life itself, in all of its dynamics. Goodness, that's a lot to join together.

Pondering the amazing language of these three passages, coming straight from the author of marriage Himself, I believe a couple of themes stand out clear and strong. Here we go, Working Man. Let's get bold and state it plainly.

The list of ideas that matter in a marriage can be long indeed, hence the complexity of the topic. But you can't do a bunch of things all at once and expect to succeed. You will fail. Back to Chapter 1. Break it down, frame it, and prioritize.

Marriage can be reduced to two clear principles, drawing straight from the statements and actions of the Almighty. If these are followed, a healthy, enduring, satisfying, and highly productive union will be the reward. The most fundamental notions of marriage are not compatibility, career fulfillment, personal satisfaction, or sexual gratification. These ideas, while very powerful and important, are actually outcomes.

Now, Working Man, let's state these two principles and build them out:

Principle 1: Commitment to the Marriage Itself

Principle 1 of a successful marriage is for each partner to have an undying, unshakable, unconditional commitment to the marriage as its own element, its own object. Each partner, beginning with dating and continuing throughout the duration of matrimony, must view the marriage as a separate entity, distinct from each individual. Once vows are exchanged, the individual is no longer what matters. It is about the unit. The marriage must be viewed as a sacred covenant, a contract of Divine origin and nature that is to be respected and held in honor.

No matter the circumstance or environment, no matter the events, no matter the cultural surroundings, the entity of marriage is sacrosanct. The emphasis is no longer about him or her once married—it is them. The union itself is what matters.

Principle 1 brings endurance to a marriage. This endurance is accomplished mostly through perspective. Every marriage should begin with reams of affection, and they often do. This affection also often fades. This first principle of marriage allows the man and woman to step back, gain perspective, and allow respect for the marriage vows to override all opposing forces. Time and perspective will conquer all forces attempting to rend a marriage asunder, as long as the context of unending, unbreakable respect for the marriage unit is maintained.

Once the idea of uncompromised, sacred commitment to a marriage is embedded in the mind of a man and a woman, all other problems take a secondary position. The man and woman then go about the business of resolving whatever issue faces them, always in the context of respect for the unit as a distinct, separate entity. If any problem in life is allowed to breach this commitment, the marriage is in jeopardy, not likely to survive.

Without this view of marriage—where the bond supersedes the components—when put under pressure, individuals will separate from the bond, and the risk of marriage failure becomes high. The commitment must come from both sides, not one or the other. Both parties, husband and wife, willfully and knowingly accept the responsibility. Domination will never work—a joint commitment is required.

Marriage is not a toy that we play with as we desire. It is an adult venture that changes your life. You will never be the same.

Humans have tried every contrivance possible to bend marriage to their own plan or selfish end. They all fail. Marriage was created with this commitment built in. It is not ours to defile, and the nature of the commitment will not be denied.

Principle 2: Solving Problems Together

Principle 2 of a successful marriage is for the man and woman to be able to solve problems together. Life really is just a series of problems coming our way. For a married couple, the ability to work through these together is the second key determinant of marital strength. Many skills, tactics, and relationship methods will be developed along the way to support Principle 2, but the basic idea is straightforward and foundational: A successful married couple will be able to approach problem-solving as a unit. You must do it together.

While Principle 1 brings endurance to a marriage, Principle 2 brings productivity and fulfillment. It is possible for a marriage to survive a lifetime following only Principle 1. However, based on observation, these marriages tend to not be very happy. A grim determination to stay the course can be effective, but there is much more to be gained in marriage than just endurance. These positive achievements, alongside longevity, come about through Principle 2.

Think back to the Scripture passages quoted to open this chapter. This Principle 2 that we discuss is Genesis 1:27–28 in practice. This is living out what God intended from the start.

These two ideas combined bring magic to a marriage. The result is a happy, healthy, lifelong marriage filled with joy, accomplishment, and meaning. The marriage becomes a separate personality, distinct from either partner, made unique by the contribution of each individual.

No two marriages will be alike, and God's inimitable, specific grace will be displayed for the entire world to see through any couple willing to make these two commitments. These principles are not hard to understand, but dedication to them must be absolute. This isn't easy, but it is highly achievable. Happiness and fulfillment beyond your most grand imagination await those who dare make the commitment. Disaster, heartache, and difficulty that can stretch across generations await those that take these concepts lightly.

Take stock, Working Man. The complexity that slaps you in the face when considering marriage is, when framed correctly, very manageable. In reality, these two principles will carry you through whatever may come. Focus on what matters. Take God's view, the moral view, and understand what you must do.

Now, get to work, my friend. Working Woman is depending on you. She needs you. Make it count.

Tips for the Wise and Romantic

Now, Working Man, allow me to give you a couple of tips. This is especially for you younger Working Men, or those of you that have hit hard times and are starting over in marriage. Maybe twice. Or three times. Some of you learn slowly.

The dating phase would be an excellent time to ask yourself questions based on the two principles above. Conduct your dating with purpose—tactfully, of course, and with class and dignity but also with a point in mind. You need to know some things. Gather information until you can honestly answer these two questions: Can I honestly and without reservation make a Principle 1 commitment to this person? Can I solve problems with this person? With kindness, get to the point and get the information that you need.

A good exercise during dating would be to practice Principle 2 as much as possible. Work through every problem you can think of. Take on challenges intentionally. It's great practice, and it's an opportunity to learn, discover, and understand the person you are next to. As you practice Principle 2, you will be better able to answer the question regarding Principle 1.

KEEP IT SOUND

Let's summarize and add a few points for clarity, strength, and encouragement. This will keep your marriage sound for a lifetime.

- "Let each individual among you also love his own wife even as himself; and let the wife see to it that she respect her husband." Ephesians 5:33

  - The verse above is a summary of verses just prior, Ephesians 5:22–32. Paul summarizes the dynamics of marriage and, in doing so, reveals the core needs of each spouse. Work to meet these following needs.

    - A husband owes his wife care and protection. She has a deep need to feel safe.

    - A wife owes her husband respect. He has a deep need to feel honored.

  - A speed limit, a governor, exists on these two obligations. In no way does marriage interfere with an individual's direct accountability to God. My spouse does not become my creator, my redeemer, or my ever-present guide. Some things can only be gained through a walk with Christ, not through a friendship or marriage. A wife respects and honors her husband, but this does not convey the status or authority of a creator to the husband. A husband loves and serves his wife, striving to meet her needs, but this does not make the wife a redeemer or object of worship. A soul can only be saved through connection with its Redeemer and Creator. No earthly substitute or intermediary can suffice.

- The fact bears repeating. This idea is vital, Working Man. I will say it again. Marriage (and family) is the only social institution instituted by God in the Garden of Eden prior to the Fall. Marriage is God's plan for mankind from the very beginning, His original plan.

- Marriage is so amazingly profound because it looks back to the very beginning of God's intentions and looks forward to the completion of God's plan of redemption (Christ and His Church, Ephesians 5:22–32).

- Marriage is a couple binding hearts and hands in the temporary here and now to join the perfection of God's will revealed in the past with the perfection of His promise for the future. It is a profound act of faith.

- Relationship conflict in marriage is unavoidable. You are just two flawed people who have made a commitment together. What matters is how you handle the conflict. See the two principles defined above.

- Cast aside a very dangerous and popular myth—that absence of conflict is the sign of a happy marriage. Nonsense. All that means is that nobody is talking to each other.

- Marriage, at its best, contains two partners offsetting and suppressing the other's weaknesses, while enhancing, highlighting, and encouraging the other's strengths. At its worst, the opposite occurs. Strengths are suppressed, and weaknesses are magnified.

- Marriage is dynamic, just like life. Watch the trend in your marriage. It will spiral up, strength upon strength, or it will spiral down, weakness upon weakness.

- Working Man, reinforce and amplify your spouse's strengths. Offset her weaknesses. And ask the same of her. Make the request explicit. Talk it through.

- The burden and obligation jointly shared by a married couple is to walk the discipleship walk together, as a united couple. The bond of marriage does not substitute for the Creator–Created relationship, but rather you choose to walk with the Creator side by side with the spouse, holding forth the closest-possible relationship known among beings of human flesh.

Chapter 4

INTIMACY: A GIFT FROM ABOVE

WORKING MAN, WE have covered the foundation of marriage, what it stands on, the bedrock, how it was created. Now, we get to the fun part. What happens when you get it right? What can you expect when you buckle down and work Chapter 3 as we have discussed? Is it just more hard work, more death and taxes, and more burdens to bear?

Hold tight, Working Man. You are about to have more fun than you ever thought possible. Fun in a deep and lasting way, not peripheral or ephemeral. This isn't skirting the edges of fun. This is in-over-your-head fun, soaked-and-saturated fun—fun down to your bones, fun from the tips of your toes to the top of your head.

We are speaking of fun that is lifelong and comprehensive. It will brighten your outlook, warm your core, put a spring in your step, and make you a satisfied man. This is fun you will never want to leave.

We are speaking of comfort that soothes and satisfies the soul. A strong marriage settles your being. It brings the fires of hearth and home right into your center. You feel it from the inside, and you know there is so much more to come.

The touch of that Working Woman's skin brings you to life. It elevates your being to new heights. You need no drugs or alcohol when you have this, Working Man. Stimulation hardly begins to describe the payoff of a Chapter 3 marriage. If you put in the work, you will catch lightning.

Bolts of lightning against a night sky give some hint of the pleasure waiting for you. Lay the foundation properly and the pleasure you will possess and enjoy defies description. Ask yourself some questions, Working Man:

- Do you think you've seen delirious pleasure?

- Do you think contentment is restricted to temporary status, dependent on circumstance?

- Do you think happiness is condemned to be a passing condition?

- Do you think sensuality has a limit?

- Do you think elation is for children only?

- Do you think romance trends down, fading with time?

- Do you think affection is wishful thinking?

- Is delight an overrated notion?

- Can adoration even apply in the adult world?

A marriage with a Chapter 3 foundation will educate you on all these points. You have no idea, Working Man. Follow with me.

The pleasure in a properly grounded marriage will not drain away and will not falter, because whatever life puts in your path, you and Working Woman know that you have each other. Each and every hardship that life piles on is just another opportunity to work together, overcome, and love each other more deeply than before, for all to see. You and Working Woman are living, breathing testimonies to the greatness of God, His Grace, and His plan. It is you, your spouse, and the Almighty against the world. You will win.

First, though, we must blow up some big lies. Our modern culture is handy that way. It lies to you, wrecks you, deceives you, promises you the moon and then turns on you, watches you crash and burn, and walks away laughing. Nice chaps, these modern culture types. They have your back, all right … as a big target.

We will begin with what I believe is the biggest lie regarding romance and marriage. It is very modern and frighteningly common. This lie picked up in the U.S. in the late 1950s and steamrolled through the 1960s. From the 1970s to now, it has embedded itself in every nook and cranny of culture. It permeates media, TV, movies, entertainment—you name it.

The big lie goes like this—sex and love can be separated and treated as independent areas of your life. The lie says that sex is for pleasure and love is for family. They may or may not abide together. It doesn't really matter. Enjoy them both. Quaint sentiment, isn't it?

The truth is this—it isn't so; they can't be separated. You can try, but grave consequences await if you do.

Sex and love are gifts from our Creator, and they were never intended to be separate. Remember, it's His plan, not yours. It's best to go with His.

Sex and love are like a finely braided rope—they are twisted together, intertwined. Sex and love are meant to dwell together, and the result is everything I described above—intimacy.

Intimacy is an emotion that fills the human heart like no other. Because it results from deliberate human action that is intentionally aligned with God's stated will and plan, the resulting satisfaction is not human. It is Divine.

Look back above at our list of questions, Working Man, and consider again. How can happiness be lasting while circumstance is unstable and threatening? How can the ideas of delight, adoration, and affection survive grade-school innocence? How can pleasure possibly be delirious and remain legal? It can happen because it flows from something beyond this world. The source is outside of circumstance.

Intimacy is God's way of saying, "I am pleased with what you do." He does not ask you to obey for no benefit. You are not working in vain. A couple that orders their steps and marriage by His eternal guidelines encounter a benefit flowing from Heaven itself.

Working Man, you can't get that any other way. You can't get it from hookers. You can't get it from illicit sex. You can't get it from passive, casual relationships. You can't get intimacy from one-night stands or pornography. Tinder doesn't have it; *Penthouse* doesn't sell it; no strip bar can put it on stage.

Why? Why can't you pull sex and love apart, grab the benefits, and drive on? Because the human heart is simply not built that way. The purpose of sex is to build and maintain a family, and a family cannot function without love. The hard work of Chapter 3 brings the immeasurable benefit of Chapter 4—intimacy. You can never have the pleasure and satisfaction outside of marriage that you can inside of marriage. If you try, you are fighting against God. Good luck.

Working Man, let's go back to Scripture and look at what the Almighty has to say. That's always a good idea. Let's go back to Paul as he wrote the Ephesians.

> Husbands, love your wives, just as Christ also loved the church and gave Himself up for her, so that He might sanctify her, having cleansed her by the washing of the water with the word, that He might present to Himself the church in all her glory, having no spot or wrinkle or any such thing; but that she would be holy and blameless. So husbands also ought to love their own wives as their own bodies. He who loves his own wife loves himself; for no one ever hated his own flesh, but nourishes and cherishes it, just as Christ also does the church, because we are parts of His body. "For this reason a man shall leave his father and mother and be joined to his wife, and the two shall become one flesh." This mystery is great; but I am speaking with reference to Christ and the church.
>
> Ephesians 5:25–32

You will be busy for a lifetime with this one, Working Man. And it is well worth it.

Paul declares some truly amazing ideas here. He references back and forth between husband and wife, and Christ and the church—"church" meaning you and I as we believe and follow Christ the Messiah. He then quotes Genesis 2:24, and adds one humdinger of a line, "This mystery is great; but I am speaking with reference to Christ and the church."

I won't pretend to know everything packed in these verses, but there are a few things I can declare from understanding and experience.

Paul states himself that the mystery is great, but there are profound truths that we can know, walk in, benefit from, and proclaim.

Working Man, marriage is the closest thing to Heaven that you will experience on this earth. Marriage is a symbol, a demonstration of what God always had in mind when He called a people to Himself. It is an earthly declaration of plans made in Heaven.

It is what occurred in the Garden of Eden for Adam and Eve when they joined together in the bond of marriage and walked with God in the cool of the day.

When you choose marriage, you choose to declare God's will on this earth. You are a living demonstration of His Grace and His creative power.

What is the result? What does God provide you in return? Intimacy. Something that fills your heart and soul, with no substitute to be found.

Working Man, do you want happiness in this life? Do you wish for satisfaction and pleasure? Do you want comfort and solace? Do you wish for heartfelt peace and accord? Here's the ticket.

Love that Working Woman with all your might. Love her with all your heart and soul. Love her faithfully with no reservation. Give her your entire being, all you have and all you will ever be. Love her the way Paul said to. "Husbands, love your wives as Christ loved the church and gave Himself up for her."

Do this, Working Man, and she will love you back. She will love you with passion and desire that shivers the timbers. You will mark no end to your pleasure and satisfaction. It will grow, multiply, expand, and fill all your days. There is nothing this secular world has on offer to match it. It took the will of Heaven to create something this good.

Marriage properly done, a Chapter 3 marriage, truly is Heaven on Earth. Working Man, if you think sexual satisfaction, a release, or an orgasm, is the only thing that matters, you are an absolute fool. That is a carnal, selfish, inward approach.

Working Woman cannot trust you if that is what you think. Working Man, consider a poignant and honest thought. What happens when that Working Woman gives herself to you sexually? Consider how vulnerable she is, how open, exposed, and unprotected she becomes, all for your benefit. She is counting on you to understand that, to respond appropriately.

If love and sex are bound together as originally intended, you will do so. You will honor the trust she offers you and give the same in return. You will be faithful.

If you don't, if an orgasm is all you care about, you will lie to yourself and call that fulfillment. You are wrong. A few hormones and endorphins won't get the job done. That type of fulfillment is a mirage, always on the horizon but never at hand, always promising, never consummated. A hormonal, emotive release is temporary and shallow compared to what is available and is, at its core, an intensely selfish act.

Plant this idea in your mind, Working Man—hormones and associated sensations were never intended to operate in a vacuum. They are not an end in themselves. Chasing hormonal release results in a rift separating lifestyle from deeper, lasting values. Values of honor, integrity, trustworthiness, dependability, and self-sacrifice become separated from who you are and how you live.

If you want better, Working Man, if you want the pleasure I speak of, then go to work on your relationship with Working Woman. Use Chapter 3 to put it into practice. Per God's promise and plan, you will touch the Divine. In the here and now, today. This is not by-and-by stuff. I mean right now, as we speak. Grab that

Working Woman, do it kindly, and love her like you mean it. Be a man—make your commitments and keep them.

You see, when Working Woman makes love to a man, she is susceptible to disease, deception, a child that she must raise alone, heartache, and the frightening idea that she has wasted her time on a man who isn't worth a cent. Don't be that man. Show some spine, Working Man, bring some character, and make Chapter 3 your own. Working Woman will love you—and make love to you—for your trouble. You will be way beyond hormones and endorphins on this one, my friend. Heaven will be yours to enjoy in the here and now. It will be no mirage.

Any man can be a jerk, a true jackass, a loser, and a philanderer. Why would you want to be that man? If you pursue this path, if you separate pleasure from those deeper values, you will find yourself unavoidably arriving in a place you will not like—you will be alone. As the old saying goes, you can choose your own actions, but you can't choose your own consequences.

Thankfully, there's better built within us. You have an innate knowledge of these eternal things we speak of here. You know Chapter 3 is correct—I've just made it plain and easy to understand. Make the noble, honorable choice and get to work. Your reward is ... Working Woman.

HEAVENLY PLEASURE

Working Man, you should be fired up at this point. All the work ahead of you has a purpose, an objective, and a reward. I want to close these two chapters on marriage and the second example of Chapter 1 with a final thought. Let's let God have the final say.

Some think Christians are prudes and backward when it comes to pleasure, both sexual and emotional. They think we don't understand what is out there. They think we are bound to rules and don't know what can be had, what can be enjoyed. This is just another cultural lie, although this one isn't strictly modern. It's been around a long time. There are modern variations, but the lie is as old as the hills.

The truth is just the opposite. We choose to follow the plan of the One who made all of this to begin with. We figure He knows best. I've seen nothing in my years to convince me otherwise.

When it comes to pleasure, listen to the God who created it. The book in the Holy Bible called Song of Solomon is a gem. It is one of the oldest romance stories ever told. I will leave studying the entirety of the tale to you, but I think it important to call out one verse—just part of a verse, actually.

As the tale unfolds between lovers, God interjects at a certain point and gives instruction that we should all follow. It is instructive to the end of time. God is speaking directly, in the first person, to the man and woman engaged in romantic affection.

> Eat, friends; Drink and imbibe deeply, O lovers.
>
> Song of Solomon 5:1b

There you have it, Working Man. God's eternal will for husband and wife, straight from His mouth for all to hear. Enjoy. "Imbibe deeply." *Aprovecho*, as my Spanish-speaking friends would say. That is God's view of sexual satisfaction.

And the world would call us prudes. Ha!! To the Working Man who scoffs at Chapter 3, I will call him Frustrated Working Man. Frustrated Working Man, go back to your strip bar and pretend. While you are trying to understand Tinder, I will be with my Working Woman, enjoying more pleasure than you will ever know—and as often as I want, because she trusts me, she loves me, and she knows that I will always be there for her.

A CRITICAL QUESTION ANSWERED

Working Man, now we return to the open question left in the second example of Chapter 1. Remember, we were discussing the problem of male infidelity in a marriage. We applied our problem-solving technique, first of all recognizing this as a moral problem requiring a moral framework. Then I asked the question: What happens, Working Man, if you object to the moral frame, considering the frame to be inadequate to the challenge of changing human action?

At the end of the problem-solving process regarding male infidelity, we realized we'd hit the ancient and persistent problem of action versus ideas. How can we be assured of actually taking action versus simply knowing the right thing to do and never doing it? We can talk all day long about the damage of male infidelity in marriage, but we need a means of making the male faithful, someone Working Woman can rely on.

Let's talk about this straight up, Working Man. We need an answer. I've waited to this point in the conversation for the purpose of first establishing the prominence and unavoidable need of a moral framework. It's popular these days to think that morality is out of date and overly restrictive, that personal preference rules over moral choice. "To each his own," as the saying goes.

That just won't do, Working Man. Many incredibly important choices in life, the most important, actually, are moral in nature. Pretending otherwise doesn't change this fact, it only makes you childish and unprepared. This isn't something Working Woman can operate with.

And so it is with this problem. The practice of faithfulness in a marriage, a single man to a single woman, is inherently a moral concept. It requires a moral frame.

You should be accustomed to this by now, Working Man. This has been a big part of our conversation so far. We go back to our bedrock, our foundation, our North Star. We will look to the God of the Holy Bible and take instruction there.

I'm going to make this simple and straightforward. Much study can go into this, and I encourage you to follow up and broaden your knowledge, Working Man, but I will state in plain terms how this is done. This results from many years of problem-solving along these lines.

If you want to be successful in an area like marriage fidelity, you have to face a hard truth, a spiritual truth. Every day when you wake up, with no exception, you face two opponents.

Both opponents want you to fail and they are stronger than you. You cannot defeat either one of them individually, let alone in combination. You have no chance. These opponents have a strategy to bring you to failure, and they actively work against this plan, every day. You are toast, destined to fall.

Unless, thankfully, there is intervention. We have hope, if we only look beyond ourselves. First, Working Man, let's define these opponents.

The first opponent is spiritual personalities wholly devoted to wickedness. In Christianity, we call this opponent Satan and his minions, demons. They plant thoughts, invoke emotions, and thereby influence actions. They are very good at it. They know your weaknesses and exploit them with expert skill.

They are not impressed by you, Working Man. They do not respond to faith, hope, love, logic, or reason. They care not for your accomplishments or your reputation. It all means absolutely nothing to them. They have no fear of you, and they know their temptations will work. They know your nature and how to manipulate it to their end.

And now we have the second opponent—you, Working Man. Yes, that's right. You are your own worst enemy. Your nature is prone to wrongdoing in many forms, including being unfaithful to Working Woman.

It's a bleak outlook. You are bent toward failure with demons relentlessly prompting you to fail. I'm afraid it's all over, Working Man. Faithfulness in marriage is a pipe dream, a hopeless venture, a mirage doomed to evaporate.

But our God prevails. Read on, Working Man. There is a reason I prompted you in Chapter 2 to embrace faith in the Almighty. There is nothing impossible with Him, and this is true with faithfulness in marriage.

You see, demons are not afraid of you, but they are terrified of Christ. He beat them on their terms and on their turf. Demons don't listen to a thing you have to say, except to exploit your words as an opening for deception and temptation, but they respond immediately to every word of Christ our Savior. His authority is absolute, and demons know it.

And authority is the only thing a demon will respond to. The word of Christ, truth, light, is their undoing. They cannot remain where the Word, the light, the truth, the authority of Christ is held high.

So, what of the other opponent—yourself? What is the answer there, Working Man? There is only one answer for the fallen, broken nature of mankind, known in Christianity as flesh. God makes it clear in His Scriptures that the only answer for the nature of flesh is death: the Crucifixion. This is a hard truth to accept, but in God's view, there is no way around it. He is holy, and we are not. It is a simple, plain, immovable fact.

Fortunately for us, we don't have to personally experience this death. God has made a way. Through faith, the death of Christ is our atonement, sufficient for both payment and restoration.

And here is the daily discipline, Working Man, the only way to face these two constant opponents and succeed. It comes down to three simple steps, the steps and walk of a disciple of Christ:

1. Take thoughts to the Word, the Scriptures.

2. Leave flesh, impulses, urges, at the Cross.

3. Don't walk alone. Don't become isolated. Walk with a friend, often a spouse.

Thoughts of every form and nature, many of which are unwholesome, will fill your mind each day. Take your mind to the Scriptures, Working Man. Think on these things. New habits will be formed, and demons will have nothing to do with them, for these new habits are steeped in God's revealed will. It's just like flipping on a light switch. Darkness flees, immediately.

Your flesh, your nature, Working Man, is hopelessly lost. You cannot reform or rejuvenate it. It must be killed, and that should be your daily mindset. Your old nature is to be taken daily to the Cross and left there. There is no other answer.

Sometimes you will get distracted. Sometimes you will want to return to old habits. Sometimes, your willpower and stamina will not be up to the task. This is understandable, Working Man. Don't become isolated. Never walk alone. Find a friend and walk together. This can be Working Woman or a close friend, another Working Man, striving to leave a legacy, just like you are.

If you practice these three steps daily, you will succeed, and Working Woman will find at her side a faithful man whom she loves with her whole heart. You have your frame, Working Man. Walk on.

ENCOURAGEMENT BY THE NUMBERS

As we close out our chapters on marriage, let's end with some good news, statistically speaking. Do you remember that near 50% lifetime-fail rate for new marriages that we discussed back in Chapter 1, in the second example on marriage and divorce? Here's something to mull over, Working Man, something to clear your mind and bring great encouragement—a pick-me-up, if you will. That 42%–50% lifetime divorce rate assumes no "other factors" are introduced. That's just a straight analysis on all marriages, in every kind of condition.

But as we've been discussing, there are things you can do, major factors of mitigation that you can bring to bear, if you have the will and mindset to get it done. As it turns out, it's not a toss-up at all. Research shows that if you work hard at it, bringing into play all the positive factors that you can, it is possible to reduce the risk of marriage failure down to a very low number. If you and Working Woman put your minds to it, you can take that risk to zero.[28]

As I said, "Walk on." And smile as you go, walk with confidence. Your problem-solving frame will work.

---

[28] Paul R. Amato, "Research on Divorce: Continuing Trends and New Developments," *Journal of Marriage and Family* 74, no. 3 (2010): 650–666, https://doi.org/10.1111/j.1741-3737.2010.00723.xhttps://doi.org/10.1111/j.1741-3737.2010.00723.x;
Matthew D. Bramlett and William D. Mosher, "Cohabitation, Marriage, Divorce, and Remarriage in the United States," *Vital and Health Statistics, Department of Health and Human Services* 23, no. 22 (2002): 1–93, https://www.cdc.gov/nchs/data/series/sr_23/sr23_022.pdf;
Sarah W. Whitton et al., "Attitudes Toward Divorce, Commitment, and Divorce Proneness in First Marriages and Remarriages," *Journal of Marriage and Family* 75, no. 2 (2013): 276–287, https://doi.org/10.1111/jomf.12008;
Glenn T. Stanton, "What Is the Actual Divorce Rate?," Focus on the Family, November 4, 2015, https://www.focusonthefamily.com/marriage/what-is-the-actual-divorce-rate/;
Maureen R. Waller and H. Elizabeth Peters, "The Risk of Divorce as a Barrier to Marriage Among Parents of Young Children," *Social Science Research* 37, no. 4 (2008): 1188–1199, https://doi.org/10.1016/j.ssresearch.2008.05.010;
R. Kelly Raley and Larry Bumpass, "The Topography of the Divorce Plateau: Levels and Trends in Union Stability in the United States After 1980," *Demographic Research* 8, no. 8 (2003): 245–260, https://doi.org/10.4054/DemRes.2003.8.8.

Chapter 5

RAISING KIDS: A COOKBOOK APPROACH

NOW, **WORKING MAN,** while you and Working Woman are enjoying each other, as you should be, kids come along. I have a warning for you—they do not present themselves with a manual.

This is a Figure 1 problem if there ever was one. You should see the pattern in our conversation by now. Here's a big issue in life. Approach it by applying the same principles from Chapter 1. Break it down, frame it, make it a Figure 2 problem, and you can solve it. If you focus on key concepts, and let principles guide you, you'll do a pretty good job.

What I want to share with you in this chapter is the frame Melissa and I worked out over the years. We applied Chapter 1 to the very intimidating task of raising kiddos, and here is how we did it.

I have one caveat to state before we get started. This frame is 100% suited to your standard-issue, neurotypical, rambunctious, rowdy bunch of kids—one or a dozen of them. However, if you are in that place of having a disabled child, you will need to add a few things. Melissa and I never walked that path, so I can't speak to it specifically. I will respectfully, and with deep appreciation, leave that to the reader.

STAGES AND OBJECTIVES

Our frame is the following. As we see it, from raising four kids and now with nine grandkids, and working alongside many friends doing the same, childhood separates into five key stages:

- Age 0–2: Infants

- Age 2–4: The Toddler Years

- Age 4–12: The Golden Years

- Age 12–18: The Teen Years

- Age 18+: Adulthood

The age boundaries are rough and will vary, hence the overlap in age breakdowns above, but there is a fairly clear break between each stage—developmental markers, if you will.

I believe you will find it helpful, Working Man, to distinguish the stages, the age groups, and define an objective for each one. There is a key goal you want to reach within each stage. Raising children is cumulative. You start with foundational things and advance as a kid is ready.

The list below gives the objective for each stage that Melissa and I used. I will expound after the list.

- Age 0–2: Infants
    - Physical care, love, and protection
- Age 2–4: The Toddler Years
    - The meaning of "no"
- Age 4–12: The Golden Years
    - Learning character and values, progressively more complex with age
    - Complete trust in mom and dad
- Age 12–18: The Teen Years
    - Testing values, making what is taught their own
    - Learning judgment and complexity
- Age 18+: Adulthood
    - Leaving the nest
    - Pursuing an independent path

Okay, Working Man, let's break these down and have more discussion on the objectives, stage by stage.

INFANTS

These are the little babies, from birth to around two years of age, 18 months at least. Physical care is intense, and all the while, this is how you say "I love you." Every touch point, every feeding, every diaper change, every nap time, every rocking session, all the giggles, the coos, the eye contact, says "I love you" to that little one.

A baby knows you love them by the way you care for them. When you engage, they know. And this is how they develop. You wrap them in love by meeting their every need. That means everything to the infant.

Physical and emotional development will largely take care of itself if you just meet their physical needs and do it in a warm, loving way. Talk to them. They are listening. Hug them, play with them, take walks, push them in the stroller, nap beside them. They notice. All of this spurs brain development, physical and emotional.

THE TODDLER YEARS

Hmmm. The terrible twos and threes—this stage is a little tougher, Working Man. They are cute, for sure. And all the fun things they do—walking, running, talking—it's all cool.

And they think you are scum. And stupid. They have found their will, and you are not worthy.

Accept your fate, Working Man. You are the moron that should do as you are told. And not by Working Woman—she is as dumb as you are. It's by the little king or queen that you dared bring into this world. They are now your boss.

All the physical care requirements still apply. Hopefully, in there somewhere, you will get them potty-trained and able to feed themselves. These are big steps. But you are still stupid, hopelessly dense.

Know this, Working Man, as you will have to address this situation. You have one goal for a toddler. By the age of four, maybe five, but don't stretch it to six, the young tyrant will have to learn what "no" means.

That is your singular goal, for them to understand that when you or Working Woman say "no," you mean it and that is the end of it.

The secular world may scoff. It often does. I've become used to this over the years. However, the little tyrants need to learn the discipline of "no" for three very big reasons:

1. Their own safety depends on it. The first time they take off running in a parking lot, you will understand what I mean.

2. Every phase thereafter, including their success in adulthood, depends on it. This lesson is the beginning of self-control. These are the seeds of understanding emotion and how to control it. If you skip this lesson, the child will not be self-governed, self-directed. If you are not in control of your emotions, you are not in control of your person. This all begins in the toddler years.

3. The sanity of the world around you, and that of yourself. You will have no friends and no mental lucidity if you do not curb the despot seated at your table.

There are worlds of techniques to get this done, Working Man. Melissa and I had our favorites. This challenge is a prime Principle 2 item, from Chapter 3. You and Working Woman must tackle this challenge together. Through problem-solving, you will find a rhythm, an articulation that is your very own. That is God's grace coming through, His unique expression through your family.

Set the objective, choose your techniques, and get it done. Be consistent. That will come through loud and clear to the Junior Stalin in the household. They will get the point.

THE GOLDEN YEARS

Personally, I think this is the sweetest time of all. All phases are grand, hear me well, but this one is special and crucial. Each and every child is a miracle from Above, made in God's own image, and all stages of development matter. This stage, though, fills a soft spot in my heart.

After the "no" issue is settled, the kids fall into a groove. They trust mom and dad. They believe you are the best thing ever. You know everything, and they depend on you.

They soak up everything you say. They watch everything you do. They learn your values, your knowledge, your character, your judgment—everything about you. They are little sponges, taking in everything around them.

This stage is the most natural of all. Just be mom and dad. Their curiosity will take care of the rest. Sure, there are discipline, rules, family chores, schoolwork, and all of that. And it's magic. You've laid the groundwork, now follow through with everyday living. As you and Working Woman move through and act out Chapters 1, 2, 3, and 4, the kids will learn what they need to know.

Make sure they see you love your wife. Age-appropriate exposure, of course, but they need to know what married love is all about. They will learn it from you. Take them to work. Ensconce them in daily life. They will love it and learn what is good and necessary.

I call this stage crucial because of what comes next.

THE TEEN YEARS

Here we go, Working Man. It starts to get serious now. All those values you taught them, all the judgment you imparted? It will now be tested.

And in their eyes, you are back to being stupid, a true know-nothing. How do you possibly remember to breathe?

It's quite an arc, isn't it? You are the savior for the infant, then you deserve the boot heel of the toddler tyrant. On to being the grand savant, the smartest person ever for your eight-year-old, then back to being a moron, all in the short time span of about 13 years. It's quite a journey.

That's parenting, Working Man. Comes with the territory.

Here is your posture for this stage, my friend—hold steady. Be calm, be firm, and be there for them. Remember the values you taught them? They are now becoming their own. The kids will test them, try them, and get their own handle on it all. It can be no other way.

They are now seeing the complexity in life, the contradictions and conundrums. They are now facing the demands of Chapter 1. Teach them the principles you read here. You taught them at a simpler level in the golden years, but now it's full on. They are ready to understand, and must face, all the factors in play.

The teen years are adulthood with training wheels. Your child is facing adult pressures, circumstance, and choices, but you are still there—and still paying the bills. The kids have close support in mom and dad. They are independent but not too much. You are still their safety net.

Jump right in, Working Man. And hold steady. And stand close to Working Woman. You will need each other.

Next comes the big one, the goal all along.

ADULTHOOD

I must make a confession. Something happened here that I did not in the least expect. The four kids that Melissa and I raised are now in adulthood, all with spouses and children of their own. At current count, we have the nine grandchildren mentioned before and are hoping for many more.

And here is what I never expected to be true, but I am bound to tell you the truth—this stage is the most difficult.

Yep, sure enough. I never thought this would be the case, but, in the end, you can't know what those young adults you set loose are going to do. They are independent, moral agents, choosing freely, as they see fit.

You are no longer in charge. You can now only play a support role. It's not easy to transition into this role, but it is a must.

There's more to say about this phase of parenting, Working Man—a lot more. But give me a minute. We need to cover the formula first. We'll get back to this in a sec.

THE FORMULA

As you go through the stages and you are working on each objective, it is helpful to put a frame around how you go about things. Here's the question: What is your guidepost, your bedrock, your North Star as you make each and every choice on how to guide your child to the desired end in each key phase?

You will notice something here, Working Man. I haven't been heavy on specific techniques. Most child-rearing guides are full of them, but I'm light on that portion for a reason.

You and Working Woman will take care of that. It's most important that you have the foundation right, the fundamental themes, and then choose techniques in the context of those themes, those that suit the preferences of you and your bride. Chapter 1 habits will lead you to whatever technique you need and favor. If you have the wrong foundation, you can choose techniques all day long, but you will still be wrong.

There are parenting techniques—much of them total garbage—to fill the sky these days. They don't have a philosophy, or frame, which fits the work or meets the challenge. You are lost before you start. Get the context right first, and then choose techniques that you like and are comfortable with.

Now we turn to a piece of the context that is paramount—the formula. Melissa and I followed a formula and applied it at each step of the way. Every choice, every interaction, each point of discipline, and each point of encouragement or instruction was informed by this idea. This formula put context around the entire effort.

The Formula: 2 Parts Love and 1 Part Discipline

> ➤ 1 Part Love—Mom and dad love you. You can always count on that.

> ➤ 1 Part Love—God loves you, He formed you in the womb, and He has a plan just for you.

> ➤ 1 Part Discipline—No means no. There is right and wrong.

This formula is simple in nature and profound in application—the best kind to have. We found the balance between love and discipline to be about right, and the primary components that you want a developing child to understand are all present within it. Think about this as you go through your parenting journey and apply it constantly. You will find yourself using and loving all kinds of techniques, things that you and Working Woman work out just for you, all custom fit to your family.

Parents often obsess over particular methods of child raising. To use the old phrase, this is missing the forest for the trees. Get the fundamentals right, and any number of methods will work. Just focus on the goal for each developmental stage and then apply the formula. These two items are vital, far more important than any one child-rearing technique.

There you have it, Working Man, a principle-based approach for that pack of children you and Working Woman will have or adopt and raise. I call it the cookbook approach. I hope you find it as useful as Melissa and I have.

CONCLUSIONS

As we close this chapter, Working Man, I want to go back to the adult phase of child-rearing. After all, that is the goal— well-adjusted, productive, happy, successful adult children. And grandchildren, don't forget about that.

As I said earlier, the adult stage, in my experience, is the most difficult and, at the same time, the most satisfying. All the challenges and difficulties that we have discussed so far in this book, your child, your precious, one-of-a-kind miracle, will face those head on, just as you have. They may or may not respond well; you never know. And you are not in charge. Your authority as a parent is now relegated to a support role.

My grandmother, who raised five children, had a saying: "When they are little, they step on your feet. When they are grown, they step on your heart." Knowing one of my uncles as I do, she knew what she was talking about.

And right along with that, it is joy and satisfaction beyond description to see them succeed. Only the relationship with Working Woman, the one you married and had these kiddos with, will surpass the supreme happiness you feel when holding your grandchildren. Watching your kids raise their families is truly sublime. The vantage point the Good Lord gives you in that experience is something to behold.

In the adult phase of child-rearing, Working Man, we need to be prepared for whatever choices an adult child may make. There is a strong fad these days of children abandoning family ties, especially parental ties. It is a disgusting trend. The fifth commandment is often ignored.

> Honor your father and your mother, that your
> days may be prolonged in the land which the
> Lord your God gives you.
>
> Exodus 20:12

Notice the stability that is inherent in the command and promise of that verse: "your days may be prolonged in the land." Family stability equates to social stability.

There appears to exist these days an entire cottage industry in the psychology profession geared toward counseling young adults, especially young female adults, that their parents are the source of their problems. Parents are convenient scapegoats. It's a cash cow for counseling professionals hungry for fees. Based on my experience, I would call it predatory.

Some recent research indicates the phenomena is of significant scope and size. It is possible that a quarter or more of families in the country today suffer the rift of estrangement.[29] The younger generation is finding new reasons and new methods to disregard the fifth commandment and abandon traditional family bonds.[30]

To a parent, the sting of adult child abandonment afflicts the heart. The cycle of treachery usually doesn't end with silence. The child often accompanies desertion of parents with every manner of vitriol, accusation, horrific claim, and bitterness, which they share with all not abiding on their list of approved individuals. The child can broadcast a very tragic tale.

The problem with the claims is that they typically are not true, or at least not accurate. Distortion travels along with outright lies, creating a package of deceit and defamation. The parent has labored through the better part of two decades, providing everything a child could ask for—love, care, comfort, family stability, guidance, character development, financial support, emotional support. The entire family package, set right in front of the child.

When a relationship with a child goes south, the parents are left empty, looking for a cause, working for resolution. All they are left with is the damage—broken relationships, lost friendships, and lost family connections.

When things go as planned, Working Man, and the kids turn out as you worked for, enjoy the fruit of your labor. Be the senior member of the family, providing the guidance and wisdom that age, experience, and status grant you. The next generations need you; they need your voice, your proven ways, and your tested

---

29   James Dean, "Pillemer: Family Estrangement a Problem Hiding in Plain Sight," *Cornell Chronicle*, September 10, 2020, https://news.cornell.edu/stories/2020/09/pillemer-family-estrangement-problem-hiding-plain-sight;
Karl Pillemer, *Fault Lines: Fractured Families and How to Mend Them* (London: Yellow Kite Books, 2021).
30   Daniel de Visé, "One Quarter of Adult Children Estranged from a Parent," *Blog Briefing Room* (blog), The Hill, July 19, 2023, https://thehill.com/blogs/blog-briefing-room/4104138-one-quarter-of-adult-children-estranged-from-a-parent/.

demeanor. Be there for them. They will love and appreciate you for it.

When things don't go as planned, take heart and remain joyful. There are abundant examples of children rejecting proper family structure, and God's kingdom is unmoved. His reign continues without end. Remember, the first child ever raised (Cain) was a murderer. That is the reality of human nature in this fallen world.

There is much to be said about the wayward adult child, Working Man. I will leave you with a few key thoughts here and hold the rest for another work, another book.

Parents owe their adult child two key things—unconditional love and their unvarnished view. Let's expound.

On the first point, you must distinguish between unconditional love and unconditional support. These are not the same, and many a parent has confused the two, to great detriment. Unconditional love, the selfless affection and concern for a child's well-being, should always be present, no matter what. God grants us this exact thing. He is faithful at all times, and His love is never removed, no matter what we do.

Support, however, is conditioned upon the actions of the individual. God does not bail me out if I act stupidly, irresponsibly, or criminally. He stands by and allows me to suffer the consequences, with the intention of permitting me to learn something proper and useful. Many wayward adult children are made worse, and the damage of their actions upon others is compounded, because parents rescue them every time, thus enabling destructive behavior.

Don't try to protect the family name, Working Man. It isn't worth protecting, and you will only make things worse. I will leave you with a saying from my father: "Your last name is no better than your last action. What you do is what matters." I can't say it better than that.

If your adult child is misbehaving, you owe it to everyone around, including the child, yourself, and Working Woman, to confront them and/or let them fail. Remember the story of the prodigal son (Luke 15:11–32). As this wayward son stormed away, destined to lay waste to all he had, the father let him fail. He did not chase after him and attempt to save the son from himself. And the father gave no regard to the family reputation.

On the second point, whenever conversation and opportunity arise, you should provide your unvarnished viewpoint to your adult child. They may not like it, they may not agree, and they certainly may not act upon it, but they should know where you stand.

Remember, Working Man, you know more than they do. You've seen more than they have. And nobody else loves that child more or knows them better than you and the Working Woman at your side. Speak from your experience. Let them hear it. More than likely, they will come around eventually to the wisdom you offer.

At the end of it, parenting is like life itself. It is full of joy, exhilaration, and amazing wonder at every stage. Each child is a miracle from Above, a unique expression of God's grace, irreplaceable and without duplicate. At the same time, like life, parenting can also be frustrating and filled with disappointment that crushes the soul. You never know how an adult child will turn.

A parent does not control the outcome. We signed up for that risk right from the start. Parenting is the book of Ecclesiastes in full measure. It is wondrous and vain at the same time. Let's heed the concluding words of the preacher and make his wisdom our own.

> The conclusion, when all is heard, is: fear God
> and keep His commandments, because this ap-
> plies to every person. For God will bring every

act to judgment, everything which is hidden, whether it is good or evil.

Ecclesiastes 12:13–14

Parents, after all is considered, in the end this is what matters—do your job. That is all you control, and God is pleased with it. That is all He asks of you. Yes, it can be vain and futile. Have kids and raise them anyway. Do it with joy, passion, and confidence. It is between you and the Almighty.

Whatever may happen, your dependency is on God, not your children. As Melissa likes to say, "If I whine and complain about my adult child not listening to me or acting as they should, God says to me, 'Yea, tell me about it.'"

God will never fail nor forsake us. We should remain faithful throughout, just as He is, regardless of the painful reality of adult-child misbehavior.

You have your frame, Working Man. Go forth and multiply.

Chapter 6

CAREER SUCCESS VIA PRINCIPLE

THIS CHAPTER IS a direct result of my journey from a farm and ranch kid with a very traditional American experience through the corporate world into private equity. I've covered the gamut from old world to new, and that is a unique and uncommon experience in today's world.

If you don't know it already, Working Man, you will discover this truism upon entering the adult workforce and being responsible for your own bills: It's hard to have a home without a livelihood. Idealism may rule early—livin' on love, etc.—but it will soon wilt. Cash is necessary, and bills must be paid. You are far better off to accept this fact and work accordingly. Let's employ the Old West cowboy saying, and get on with it: "We are burnin' daylight."

However, it is unwise to engage in the work world arrogant and full of ignorance. You will be mauled. Arrogance and ignorance are a combination of traits that you will come across often, unfortunately, and the result is always the same: disaster. Save yourself the trouble and stock up on knowledge. Approach the workforce and your career via the problem-solving principle, like everything else we are discussing in this book, and then you, and everyone around you, will be well served.

HISTORICAL CONTEXT

When considering the modern workforce and what is required for success, it is of great value to understand historical context. What you see in front of you did not spring up uninitiated. The forces of history have shaped what you engage with today.

Economic development has been long, difficult, uncertain, and yet amazingly successful. There are reasons for this, and understanding these forces and patterns is critical for career success. You don't need to learn the same lessons via hard knocks when history places those lessons directly in front of you. Look, ponder, and learn. Life goes better that way.

One of the better books you will read on the history of economic development is an older text, written by Dr. Friedrich Baerwald.[31] I recommend it. With apologies to Dr. Baerwald for injuries to his prose, I will take the liberty of summarizing his central idea in Figure 3.

---

[31] Friedrich Baerwald, *History and Structure of Economic Development* (Scranton, PA: International Textbook Company, 1969).

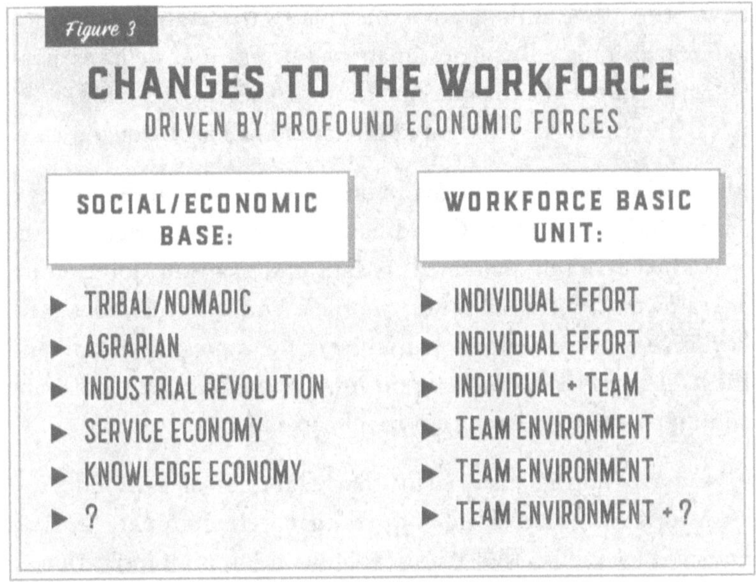

STAGES OF ECONOMIC DEVELOPMENT

Figure 3 proposes a general model of economic development. Many modern nations have followed this pattern over centuries. It is the path of humankind. The economic phases on the left are accompanied by demands on the workforce and, therefore, demands on the skill sets of wage earners, listed to the right.

The idea is straightforward, Working Man. In early human history, tribes and nomadic existence were dominant. Hunting and fishing were the staples of life. As farming, the intentional cultivation of crops and livestock, provided a more stable and abundant food supply, mankind moved to an agrarian existence. This brought towns, cities, and trade. These first two phases, from a time standpoint, reign supreme over human history. Many thousands of years were devoted to these two phases exclusively.

The next three phases, all modern, are brief by comparison. Much historical debate is given to the starting point for the Industrial

Revolution. One authoritative voice places the beginning in 1760 in Great Britain.[32] By any estimate of a beginning, we have many millennia in tribal and agrarian economies versus about 260 years since. The condensed and rapid rate of change is obvious.

Also notice the primary demand on the workforce in the first two phases: individual effort. Coordination certainly occurred, but the individual was self-contained in skill and exertion. Joint effort, or teamwork, in daily life was sporadic and informal, localized. Primitive collective efforts could be highly impressive in skill and effect, such as the Roman legion in siege warfare,[33] a Comanche raiding party,[34] or Phoenician naval capability.[35]

It is worth noting historically that examples of early effective teamwork tend to indicate cultures that were dominant in their time and locations. This historical observation is an indication or marker of things to come. However, formal, organized effort and skill, most commonly recognized in factory-based manufacturing work, was yet to come. But arrive it did and with great effect.

The Industrial Revolution came as an unstoppable economic force, bringing with it profound social impacts and changes to the workforce. Specialization was now the name of the game, with emphasis on specific production skills and coordination with

---

[32] T.S. Ashton, *The Industrial Revolution, 1760–1830*, 2nd ed. (New York: Oxford University Press USA, 1998).

[33] Jon Guttman, "Hallowed Ground: Masada, Israel," *Military History* 40, no. 4 (Spring 2024): 76–77;
Neil Faulkner, "Apocalypse," *History Today* 52, no. 10 (October 2002): 47–53;
Josh Levithan, *Roman Siege Warfare* (Ann Arbor, MI: The University of Michigan Press, 2016).

[34] S.C. Gwynne, *Empire of the Summer Moon: Quanah Parker and the Rise and Fall of the Comanches, the Most Powerful Indian Tribe in American History* (New York: Scribner Book Company, 2011).

[35] Mark Cartwright, s.v. "The Phoenicians—Master Mariners," *World History Encyclopedia*, April 28, 2016, https://www.worldhistory.org/article/897/th e-phoenicians---master-mariners/;
George Rawlinson, *The Story of Phoenicia* (New York: G.P. Putnam's Sons, 1896), 72–88, 129–139, 175–180. Original print copy held at Cornell University Library.

others possessing separate and compatible specialized skills. The manufacturing assembly line was born, and the world—and the workplace—would never be the same. Nonnegotiable, organized, and enforced teamwork was here to stay, and small- to large-team organization and middle management were born.

Next on the scene as a major economic and social force was the service sector. As disposable income rose, consumers chose to pay for services they would heretofore have performed themselves. Eating out at restaurants is the classic example. This phenomenon created an entire category of economic activity. The service sector was officially recognized in the modern economy when McDonald's fast food restaurant company (McDonald's Corporation) joined the S&P 500 stock index. McDonald's was founded in 1940 in San Bernardino, California,[36] and was added to the S&P on June 24, 1970.[37]

The service sector of our modern economy is large, expansive, and rapidly growing. It encompasses banking, financial services, education, housekeeping, transportation, entertainment, and much, much more. These many services, which we take for granted today, were trivial and nonexistent a few hundred years ago. Wealth creation and open, free markets make it all possible. In 1839, the U.S. service sector was fairly new, measurable, and small, though growing.[38] By the early 21ˢᵗ century, the service sector was fully 75% of the U.S. economy and continuing to grow its share of gross domestic product (GDP)[39] (Appendix, Figure 13).

---

[36] Eric Reed and Dominic Diongson, "History of McDonald's: Timeline and Facts," The Street, Nov 9, 2023, https://www.thestreet.com/markets/history-of-mcdonalds-15128096.

[37] Bruce Schachne (chief commercial officer at Dow Jones S&P Indices), email message to author, March 29, 2024.

[38] Robert E. Gallman and Thomas J. Weiss, "The Service Industries in the Nineteenth Century," in *Production and Productivity in the Service Industries*, ed. Victor R. Fuchs (New York: NBER, 1969), 287–381.

[39] "U.S. Real Gross Output by Industry," U.S. Bureau of Economic Analysis, September 28, 2023, https://www.bea.gov/data/industries/gross-output-by-industry.

And notice again the impact on the workforce, on you as an individual. There is a big change here, Working Man. Teamwork is now nonnegotiable. Try working at a bank with no interaction or shared duties among colleagues. You will soon find yourself unemployed. You could go for weeks with farmwork in the 1600s and not see another person. Your effort could be self-contained. Those days faded with the rise of the Industrial Revolution and ended emphatically with the arrival of the Service Sector Economy.

Possessed knowledge has always been important. From the intentional use of fire to the discovery of human flight and on to electromagnetic currents and microbiology, knowledge is critical. The formal and legal boundary of proprietary knowledge, however, is a different matter. This is a recent development with massive economic implications.

I can't say it better than Peter Drucker. Let's absorb his words of wisdom:

> The new technologies are not "applied science." Neither the modern mathematics of symbolic logic nor the perception of configuration is what is normally called "science." Yet both are central to the new technologies and, as a result, to the new industries. This is something new, something that sets the new industries sharply apart from those of the first half of this century. The technology of the twentieth century embraces and feeds off the entire array of human knowledges, the physical sciences as well as the humanities. Indeed in these new technologies there is no distinction between the two. In these new technologies the split between the universe of matter and the universe of the mind—the split

> introduced into Western thought by Descartes 300 years ago—is being overcome.[40]
>
> Knowledge has become productive. The systematic and purposeful acquisition of information and its systematic application, rather than "science" or "technology," are emerging as the new foundation for work, productivity, and effort throughout the world.[41]

Heed the words of a sage, Working Man. The blending of the physical world and the human mind—that is the beating heart of the Knowledge Economy. It will only grow in influence. It is not going away. Drucker spoke in reference to the 20th century and prior. The 21st century is proving his point emphatically. Knowledge is productive. It pays. There will be no end to these facts.

Throughout my banking career, I would instruct my teams with these words: "Banking is an information game. Whatever player obtains the best information and uses it most effectively at providing top-quality products and top-notch services to clients will win." I stand by my words, and they hold true for many industries beyond banking.

With the prominence and formative, creative, disruptive power of the Knowledge Economy has come a legal framework to support it. Intellectual property rights are not new. They reach back at least to 1474. The oldest-known formal patent process is the Venetian Patent Statute created by the Republic of Venice on

---

[40] Peter F. Drucker, *Age of Discontinuity: Guidelines to Our Changing Society*, 3rd ed. (Piscataway, NY: Transaction Publishers, 2000), 38–39.

[41] Drucker, *Age of Discontinuity*, 266.

March 19, 1474.[42] Patent rights defined in this document continue today, although the scope and breadth are beyond anything imaginable in that day and time.

Intellectual property rights (IPR) are dynamic, rapidly changing to fit the times, and rest upon a deep foundation.[43] IPR are driven by the facts stated above, that which you see all around you—knowledge is both power and money. The property of the mind as an economic factor will endure, driven by gains in productivity.[44]

So, Working Man, let's ask the question again about the right-hand side of the column in Figure 3, the workforce. We see clearly the impact of the Knowledge Economy, but what does that mean for requirements in the workforce?

The answer resonates with perfect clarity—teamwork is a requirement. You won't get much done by yourself. Those days are over, long gone.

As you build technical skills suited to engage the mixture of Industrial Revolution, Service, and Knowledge Economies, you should squarely face what working in the current economic environment means, what demands are placed upon you as an individual. You will also need skills and abilities suited to a teamwork environment. You must be a team player.

As stated early in this chapter, my personal experience is rare these days in that I've worked and directly participated across the phases listed above. I grew up on a family farm in north

---

[42] Joanna Kostylo, "Commentary on the Venetian Statute on Industrial Brevets (1474)," in *Primary Sources on Copyright (1450–1900)*, ed. L. Bently and M. Kretschmer, (Cambridge, UK: Arts & Humanities Research Council, 2008), https://www.copyrighthistory.org/cam/tools/request/showRecord.php?id=commentary_i_1474.

[43] Graham Dutfield, *Intellectual Property Rights and the Life Science Industries* (Abingdon, Oxfordshire: Routledge, Taylor and Francis Group, 2003).

[44] John Houghton and Peter Sheehan, "A Primer on the Knowledge Economy," (working paper no. 18, Centre for Strategic Economic Studies (CSES), Victoria University of Technology, Melbourne City, Australia, February 2000).

Texas. The farming methods were modern, to be sure, by 1970s to 1990s standards. Even still, in adulthood, we could go many days without direct interaction with others. The work was very much individual, stand-alone. Coordination could be done quickly and sporadically if required, but the work was up to the individual. Middle management, close direct supervision, or team coordination was unheard of.

Then came the Oklahoma State University phase, the banking career, private equity venture, and the manufacturing company. This full life-work experience effectively took me through the Agrarian Economy, Industrial Revolution, Service Sector Economy, and Knowledge Economy transitions. The journey has shaped my view, to say the least, and is a major reason for this writing.

In the production farm economy, the incentives are as simple and straightforward as you will find. If you don't work, you don't eat. You either complete work tasks on time and in a quality fashion, or your revenue suffers directly. Your revenue may suffer anyway. Risks are high—markets, weather, disease, drought—many things can go wrong. Melissa and I grew up this way and started a family in this incentive environment.

Then came the corporate world. To put it mildly, incentives are not nearly as straightforward. Many of you reading this book know exactly what I mean. Taking this walk through the workforce, observing firsthand the radical differences in behavior, and striving to achieve business results in a pressure-packed environment forced me to think deeply.

When I looked around me in the average corporate environment I could not believe what I observed—so much wasted and counterproductive effort. Lack of focus, petty agendas, political stunts, backroom shadiness, incompetence sugarcoated as leadership, deception in numerous forms—all of it detracting from our real goal: achieving a business plan.

And now, of course, we have the diversity clowns. This was taking hold as I made my way through the corporate scene. Today, unfortunately, it reigns supreme. The wokesters have outdone themselves.

Many of you will know exactly what I mean by "diversity clown" and "wokester." If you've worked with one, you don't soon forget. To provide clarity for all, I'm referring to the diversity, equity, and inclusion crew.[45] A few decades back, we referred to them as bean counters.

The term "bean counter" originated in accounting departments many decades ago, referring to the practice of counting inventories, products, widgets, everything in sight—probably beans included. When human resources personnel began doing the same thing with people, counting every divisible group based on various personal characteristics, the term was borrowed from accounting, obviously intended as a derogatory reference.

The labels have changed, but the actions are the same—an obsession with all things class, race, ethnicity, etc. In other words, focus on everything except what actually matters—productivity, skills, business plan, and goals.

There is a way through, Working Man. Keep reading.

My response to what I observed was to do exactly what I'm encouraging you to do. Look for themes, foundational ideas, bedrock. Work against this frame. The following paragraphs will show you what I found to be true and helpful.

---

[45] "What Is Diversity, Equality, and Inclusion?," McKinsey & Company, August 22, 2022, https://www.mckinsey.com/featured-insights/mckinsey-explainers/what-is-diversity-equity-and-inclusion.

THE FUTURE

As we transition to the workforce of the future, the logic of history, reading top to bottom, signifies mighty forces of economic development that will not stop. What are the chances that we reverse course and move back up that ladder? Some groups try to take us there, always with disastrous results, usually accompanied with bloody massacre, starvation, and cruelty beyond imagination.

Take a hard look, Working Man, at Pol Pot's regime in 1970s Cambodia, the Khmer Rouge rebels, and the Angkar government they established. "Year Zero" was their policy goal, a return to tribal and agrarian utopia, so they proclaimed. What they accomplished was to murder over two million of their countrymen and bring depravity to an entire civilization.[46] Socialism has a very predictable end. The setting aside of individual civil liberties and property rights cannot and will not end well. It never has, and it never will.

No doubt, there will be hiccups, setbacks, and more than a few madman troublemakers along the way, but progress top to bottom on that left-hand side of Figure 3 will continue. As Dr. Baerwald instructs, "History discloses a fact that must be learned at the very start of any study of economic development: there has never been a sustained period of uninterrupted general economic progress."[47]

Dr. Baerwald's statement is true. And history also shows that economic development, even with horrific and staggering interruptions, runs in one direction—toward improvement. Human nature drives and demands it. The economic forces involved are strong, enduring, and undeniable.

---

[46] Dith Pran and Sydney Schanberg, *Killing Fields* (London: Weidenfeld & Nicolson, Ltd., 1984).

[47] Friedrich Baerwald, *History and Structure of Economic Development* (Scranton, PA: International Textbook Company, 1969), 5.

So, back to the present question: Where do we go from here?

Personally, Working Man, I believe the economy is headed straight for space—outer space, that is. We will leave our planet and explore this amazing universe en masse. The evidence and activity are already in place.[48] Earth will be our base but no longer exclusively our home. The moon and Mars, and many places beyond, will be common for human habitation. And, of course, economic opportunities will drive all of it, with the usual legal, cultural, and business changes required to make it happen. We can't know as we stand here what all of those will be, but they will occur by way of necessity and innovation, just as humans have always effected up to this point.

So, let's ask our question again: Whatever economic driver may fill that next line in the left-hand side of Figure 3, what will the impact on the right hand side be? What demands will be imposed on the workforce? I say this in full confidence: It will be dominated by teamwork. You can place your bets elsewhere if you like, but the odds are severely against you if you do. Teamwork is here to stay.

The teamwork-oriented workforce has demands, but also immense opportunities. Leadership is required more than ever, and the financial returns to these leadership skills are also higher than ever and will continue to rise.

In my own experience, the leadership challenge is quite complex. For today's business plans, the level and type of talent and skill on a typical team is broad, diverse, and oftentimes conflicting. Backgrounds, desires, values, views, and end goals differ wildly and seldom naturally mesh. At the very least, human ambition can impose unhealthy dynamics on any team in a flash.

---

[48] Mike Wall, "SpaceX's Starship Will Go Interstellar Someday, Elon Musk Says," Space.com, March 18, 2024, https://www.space.com/spacex-starship-go-interstella r-elon-musk-says.

As a business owner or a person at any level of management, or any participant in the modern workplace, for that matter, you face a very intricate, dense, even convoluted challenge, a tough challenge requiring leadership that is up to the task. In fact, if you think about it, you face a Figure 1 problem, a blob—a challenge that is undefined, threatening, uncertain, and full of risk. You face business risk, both global and domestic, rapidly changing market environments, and rising costs of supplies, including the scarcity of production materials and labor difficulties. The list goes on.

Working Man, have you ever left for work in the morning wondering what was going to happen that day? Wondering how you could possibly get past that day's problems? You are not alone. Every free-minded person, those wanting to build their own independent life, will face the same. Let's take the challenge on intelligently, with purpose.

With a complex challenge such as this, we must return to the principles of Chapter 1, principles that show us how to conquer complexity. Let's break the leadership challenge down into its basic components. Let's simplify, frame the challenge, and work against the frame, not the blob. Make it a Figure 2 problem. Our principles are up to the challenge. Let's demonstrate.

With my experience in the simpler individual-effort workforce, I pondered the team dynamic with great curiosity. Knowing that I had to succeed in driving business results within a teamwork frame, I developed a measurement index for use in management based on one key idea: focus on fundamental human behavior without reference to titles or organizational status.

The first thing you notice when you walk into an organization are titles, what position or rank people hold. However, this makes no difference, and is often inversely related to the actual performance of a business. What drives results? It's not a person's title. It is the behavior of people on a team. Working Man, that's where you either get it done or fail. Fundamental human behavior is the key. So, how can this be harnessed and managed to achieve business goals? I have a proposal, one I used to great effect. I hope you discover the same effectiveness.

THE IMPACT INDEX

As mentioned above, personally making the transition from an individual-effort working environment to the enforced team environment compels you to notice a few things. I saw the need to create and manage a high-performing team, with all the challenges that involved. I needed a frame, so over time, I created and applied the Impact Index.

I wanted the ability to quantify a good worker, a good team member, and I could not draw my attention away from the dynamic of how ambition and competency interact—what someone aims to do against what they are capable of achieving. I observed the importance of balancing those properly. If people are dreamers who wish for and promise the moon and stars but don't deliver, that's a problem, and if people are capable of more but don't dig deeper and ask more of themselves, that's a problem too.

Your best results come with people that have balanced those two factors—ambition and capability. These folks can get things done and, importantly, can work with others to get things done.

Your ambition should be unbounded. Nobody should ever tell you what you can or can't do. You should decide for yourself and believe that the sky's the limit—be big and bold! That's the secret to America, Working Man. That is what makes us different, unique in the world and human history.

In America, no matter what situation you were born into, no matter who your parents are, the sky is truly the limit. You are not bound by family name, family station, the opinions of others, location, or associations. You are bound by you. What boundaries have you set, Working Man? Make them big, broad, audacious.

But there's a catch—can you do it? Can you get it done? Because in a modern team environment, if you fail, you're not the only person going down. Others will suffer with you, often at great loss. There are people around you who are depending on you to get something done and deliver.

If you were a buffalo hunter in the 1870s, you took great risks by striking out on the plains. One mistake could end your life. Even if you did everything right, risk of severe loss was always at hand. But it was just you. You were taking chances with your own being.

Roll forward a century and some to the modern financial world. Contrast the buffalo hunter with Ken Lay and Jeff Skilling, CEO and CFO respectively, of Enron Corporation. Lay and Skilling took great chances as well. They were bold and audacious; the sky was their limit. They were also dishonest, corrupt, and criminal. Their illegal schemes, concealed from view, inflicted substantial harm on many people.[49]

And they are not alone: Bernie Ebbers of WorldCom, Dennis Kozlowski at Tyco International, Richard Scrushy from HealthSouth, and Bernie Madoff, founder of Bernard L. Madoff Investment Securities.[50] This list goes on. The path to modern ruin is well worn.

---

[49] Peter Bondarenko, s.v. "Enron Scandal," *Encyclopedia Britannica*, last modified February 12, 2024, https://www.britannica.com/event/Enron-scandal;
Brian Cruver, *Anatomy of Greed: Telling the Unshredded Truth from an Enron Insider* (New York: Carroll and Graf Publishers, 2002);
Bethany McLean and Peter Elkin, *The Smartest Guys in the Room* (London: Penguin Books, 2004).

[50] Adam Hayes, "The Rise and Fall of WorldCom: Story of a Scandal," Investopedia, last modified August 29, 2023, https://www.investopedia.com/terms/w/world-com.asp;
Adam Hayes, "The Biggest Stock Scams of Recent Times," Investopedia, last modified November 29, 2021, https://www.investopedia.com/articles/00/100900.asp.

You see the challenge and the basic idea, Working Man. Now, let's build out the frame, a frame that is adequate to deal with scoundrels like those mentioned above. Believe me, they can be taken down before they cause so much damage. Trust me and read on.

As we build out this framework for managing performance, there is a point that I believe deserves sharp emphasis. Look carefully at that list above of corporate and business disasters. You can do further research and lengthen the list, then study them all. Notice a very important point, true in every case. By the time governmental authorities or law enforcement were involved, the damage was already high. That is commonly true. The law comes in after the fact, playing cleanup.

However, think about who was involved and when. Ken Lay was a criminal long before the law caught up with him. Who was there? Who had evidence and observations that could have been used to prevent him doing what he did?

Look in the mirror, Working Man. It's you and people like you. It's me and the people I work with. We need to be trained to know what to look for and what to do when we see it.

Read the rest of this chapter carefully. I'm about to place in your hands a tool that can be used to take the next Ken Lay down while the damage is manageable. The Richard Scrushy that you work with can be stopped and shown the door. You need the knowledge that brings the confidence to take action, action of prevention.

You are about to get that knowledge. You see, Working Man, for every Ken Lay and Bernie Madoff, there are dozens of colleagues and associates around them who saw signs of trouble, and did nothing. Don't be that colleague. Be aware, be informed, and be ready to take action. Read on.

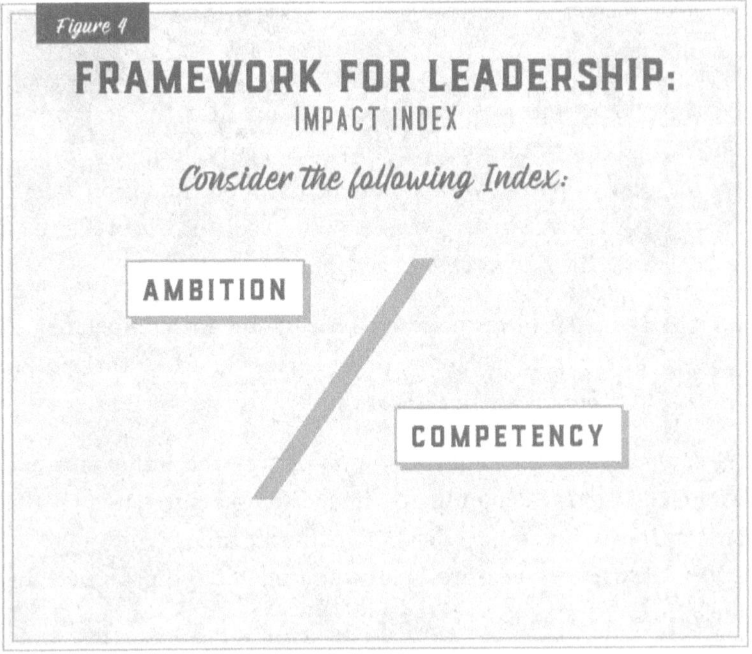

THE IMPACT INDEX

Let's start with the basic components mentioned above, a simple ratio as presented in Figure 4. First, imagine ambition and competency as separate, individual numbers, measurements on the normal numerical scale. A higher number for ambition means a person with stronger drive to achieve and higher, more aggressive goals. A lower number means the opposite—less drive, lower goals.

The number for competency is similar. A higher number means higher skill, higher capability, a person who can do more than the next. A lower number is also the opposite, just as with ambition. This person has lower skill and can do less than the next.

Now, divide the two numbers: ambition on top, divided by competency. The resulting index, the Impact Index, is a ratio, a percentage. The Index expresses ambition as a percentage of competency.

Let's continue with a hypothetical example for the purpose of clarity. Imagine a scale of 1–10 that measures ambition: 10 is high and 1 is low. A person with a score of 10 on our ambition scale is Steve Jobs or Elon Musk. A person with a score of 1 is, well, we all know a few. They don't care to accomplish much.

Let's imagine we have the same scale, 1–10, for competency. A score of 10 is Einstein. A score of 1 is Elmer Fudd, or that person whose intellect you are not impressed by. You get the idea.

Now, divide the two numbers, ambition as the numerator and competency as the denominator. If a person measures an 8 on ambition and a 4 on competency, their Impact Index score is 2.0, or 200%. If a person measures 6 on ambition and 9 on competency, their Impact Index score is 0.67, or 67%.

You can run out all the combinations, Working Man, and I think numerically you see how the Impact Index works. Two key factors should be pointed out here:

- The numbers for ambition and competency should be assessed separately. They do not necessarily move together, and they absolutely are not the same number. A person can be as smart as a whip and completely unmotivated or the opposite. They may be of average intelligence but driven like nothing you have ever seen.

- The ratio, the index, becomes its own assessment, separate from ambition or competency. The ratio carries its own characteristics and interpretation.

Figure 5 below restates the Index in intuitive form. The same concepts of measurement apply as in our hypothetical example above.

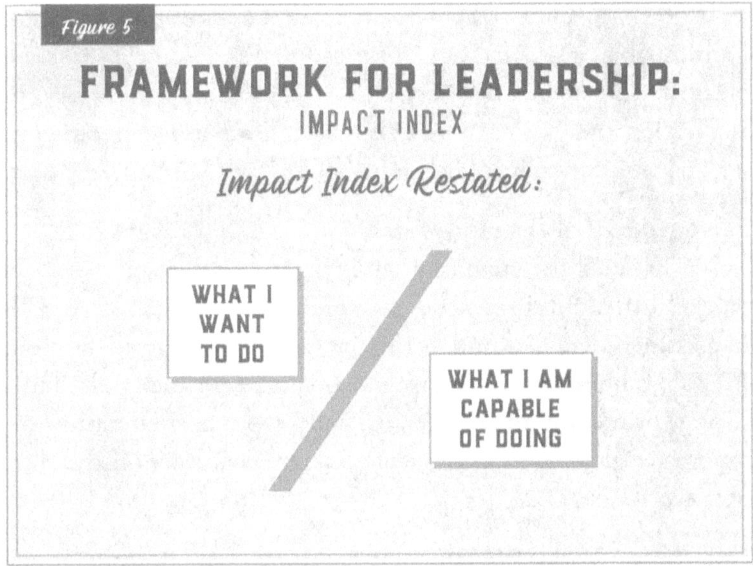

THE INTUITION OF THE IMPACT INDEX

A powerful feature of the Impact Index in Figures 4 and 5 is the ability to apply it formally or informally. A formal application requires creating two numerical measurements: one for ambition and one for competency. Then place these two measurements on the same min-to-max scale and divide the two numbers—numerator divided by denominator—to give a ratio. The measurements can be customized or taken by using tools that are already available. Many IQ tests will satisfy the need for a quick empirical measurement of capability (competency).

Two modern, very common IQ tests are the Wechsler adult intelligence scale[51] and the Woodcock–Johnson IV tests of cognitive

---

[51] Gomaa Said Mohamed Abdelhamid, Marwa Gomaa Abdelghani Bassiouni, and Juana Gómez-Benito, "Assessing Cognitive Abilities Using the WAIS-IV: An Item Response Theory Approach," *Journal of Environmental Research and Public Health* 18, no. 13 (2021): 6835, https://doi.org/10.3390/ijerph18136835.

ability.[52] Both can test the measurement of competency, or "what I am capable of doing." Organizations may, and often do, create measurements for specific jobs or business units. This is a custom application and can be quite extensive and expensive, although it may be required to meet the need.

The other half of the ratio—ambition, or "what I want to do"—can be handled the same way, with custom measurement or tools off the shelf. An off-the-shelf example is the Grit Scale.[53] Similar tools can be created and scaled to need in a custom fashion. Academic interest in measuring a personal trait like ambition is strong, providing an intellectual and empirical foundation for innovative, custom measurement and possibly future off-the-shelf options.[54]

Note here, Working Man, that the formal application of the Impact Index is possible, and powerful, but the most common use I found for this approach is informal. A subjective analysis by a manager provides insight into potential for team members and their training needs to achieve a goal. As we look closer at the use of the Impact Index, both formal and informal applications become clear.

---

[52] Fredrick A. Schrank, "Introducing the Woodcock-Johnson IV," Houghton Mifflin Harcourt, accessed March 2, 2024, https://www.hmhco.com/-/media/sites/home/hmh-assessments/clinical/woodcock-johnson/pdf/wjiv/wj_iv_author_newsletter_winter_2014.pdf?la=en.

[53] Angela L. Duckworth et al., "Grit: Perseverance and Passion for Long-Term Goals," *Journal of Personality and Social Psychology*, 92, no. 6 (2007): 1087–1101, https://doi.org/10.1037/0022-3514.92.6.1087.

[54] Andreas Hirschi and Daniel Spurk, "Striving for Success: Towards a Refined Understanding and Measurement of Ambition," *Journal of Vocational Behavior* 127 (April 6, 2021): 103577, https://doi.org/10.1016/j.jvb.2021.103577.

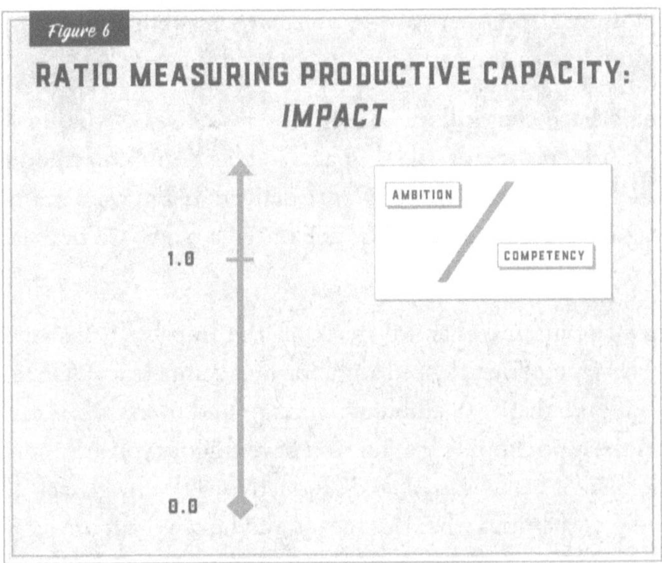

THE EMPIRICS OF THE IMPACT INDEX

Let's look closely at the application. Observe Figure 6 and think through what this number means. As in our hypothetical example above, ambition is the top number, divided by competency, which is the denominator. The ratio will be bound at the bottom by zero, assuming neither number is below zero. Some of you may object and say, "I know a few of those! Negatives, for sure!" Granted, there can be some terrible ambition and capability out there, but if you get your scale right, they will represent the bottom of the pile. Assume you have bottomed out with your measurement scale, and if/when that special employee proves you wrong, adjust! Also, obviously, you cannot divide by zero, so the capability measurement will be scaled accordingly.

There is no cap on top, it is unbounded, just as ambition should be. Dream as big as you want, with no limits, no restraints. The sky itself should not be able to limit your dreams. Once you've done that, once you've crafted a master plan to rule the universe and possess all known wealth, you have an obligation to match that dream with the capability to get it done.

Develop both the skill and the ability to deliver, Working Man. This is the power of the Impact Index. Ambition should be checked by only one thing: Can I deliver? If I'm on a team, my colleagues depend on me. They don't need a blowhard or a slacker. They need me to perform.

Somewhere around that 1.0 mark on the Impact Index indicates that I have properly balanced ambition and competency. As the ratio grows higher than 1.0, ambition outstrips and overwhelms capability. As the ratio drops below 1.0, you have abilities you are not using, latent talent is being wasted, and productivity is lost from lack of use. Let's dig deeper into what this means and how we can use it.

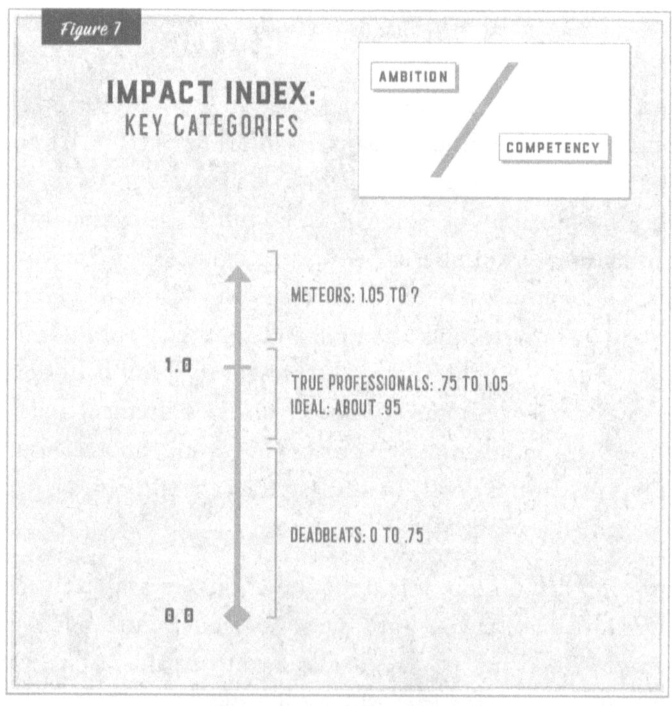

IMPACT INDEX KEY CATEGORIES

Focus on Figure 7. The Impact Index allows me to identify three key groups in any work environment. I call them meteors, true professionals, and deadbeats.

Begin with the undesirable, but always present, types of employees: those at either end of the Index. A meteor has grand visions, magnificent dreams, and usually very high self-regard. They are often charismatic and well spoken. The only problem? They don't deliver; they can't get the work done. They leave their teammates hanging. They don't carry their load. The end result is always the same: a disaster.

This is why I've coined the label "meteor." It's very impressive in flight, but a crash or burnout is unavoidable. The only open question is what the damage will be in the end. They always burn out and hit the ground, and who else is hurt along with them? How much waste and collateral damage occur? It can be substantial.

Meteors are a direct and present danger to your team or organization. They hide their true intentions as long as you allow it, and they take the organization down their predetermined path of failure as far as they can. They don't check or rein themselves in. Typically, they have no shame. After failure occurs, they look for the next gig, the next scam, the next sucker organization that will let them play.

In our Impact Index framework, Working Man, Ken Lay and Jeff Skilling, and all like them, are meteors. They are impressive for a while, but they will fail at great cost to others. But here is something most people never notice—for every Ken Lay or Jeff Skilling, there are a thousand like them who aren't famous. They are on small teams, specific departments, military units, civic boards, and the like. Their end points are just as damaging, even though the splash isn't as public.

If you want to get something done in life, Working Man, you will meet them. They will be in your company and on your team, threatening your income. What will you do? Will you even recognize them? How should you respond and prepare? Read on.

Let's look at the next undesirable group. The deadbeat is a master at hiding. They have plenty of talent—most of it unused. They are looking for a paycheck and a way to do as little as possible. As opposed to a meteor, the deadbeat's failure to deliver is not caused by lack of ability but rather lack of focus, effort, or determination—a lack of obligation to produce.

These are also deadly to a team or organization through wasted resources. Your expense line will grow, but your revenue line will not. Whereas with a meteor you will crash and burn in spectacular fashion, deadbeats cause a slow and lethal fade-out. Nonetheless, your team is done for in the end, your business plan and organization destroyed, left in ruins.

I draw the line on the ratio at 1.05 and above for meteors. Why the .05 allowance? Some people like to run hot. They don't want to leave anything on the table, no opportunities lost or untried. I grant them that. Personally, I like the ratio of .95, just to be safe. I don't want to disappoint my teammates because I don't know what I'm talking about. I want to be sure. I'm conservative in that way. Some run more out on the edge, freewheeling without going to full danger zone meteor. I say, "Fair enough." Just don't get carried away with it. I respect some differing preferences on that point and therefore draw the line at 1.05. There is a natural level of uncertainty in life, and I prefer to account for that, and help my teammates, by being sure of my own contribution.

I draw the line at .75 and below for deadbeats. Some would argue that is too low, that the standard should be higher, say maybe .9 or so, or at least .8 or above. I prefer to leave some room for a learning curve. Team members need a little room to learn and adjust.

You can tighten the standard here some if you like; just don't be too harsh. People need room to grow and improve.

Failure is one of the great learning opportunities in life, and we all need room to experience it. Don't be unrealistic, and most importantly, don't be more demanding of others than you are of yourself. I have found a boundary of roughly .75 to be a proper balance of those considerations.

If you want to be scientific about it, conduct a cost-benefit analysis to determine the boundary that your organization can afford. Assign the expected expense and revenue associated with a particular job position, providing the net margin for a job contribution. Then factor the revenue down by percentages until you reach a break-even point, or a baseline, the lowest acceptable level of return for that position. There you have your boundary, the highest amount of "laziness" that you can afford.

Now, Working Man, we turn to the prime, top-notch employees, the ones you really want to see. What makes a team high impact, high performance, is a group of true professionals, that group in the middle on the Impact Index. These folks have strong ambitions, which they match with skill and ability. They can deliver. These groups achieve wonders. They will leave you in awe at their triumphs. That .75 to 1.05 range on the Impact Index is golden and can make you very wealthy. That is a manager's and business owner's dream.

Diversity of talent, background, and views is not a problem in a team of true professionals. It is a strength. They don't care about differences. They focus on the goal, the business plan, and the objectives, then they lock arms with people around them and get it done. High achievement is a mild description for what they accomplish.

Every team manager and every business owner should have one goal with their personnel: to build a team of true professionals.

Teamwork is not an option; it is a requirement for any plan you may have. There is little need, little space, for sole contributors. Those days are long past and not likely to return. A high-performing team is your best and only chance at success. The Impact Index paints a clear picture. Your personnel-management practices (hiring, retention, termination, performance management) should focus on minimizing the top and bottom groups (meteors and deadbeats) and maximizing the middle group (true professionals).

Figure 8 below gives a rough estimate of the percentage of the workforce in each group. This is based on personal experience and reflects what I have seen in the workplace. I know of no formal research or measurement. Approximately, I have found 10%–15% of employees in each of the meteor and deadbeat groups, with 70%–80% in the center as true professionals.

There is also some intuitive logic to support these numbers. A country does not become the world's largest and most innovative economy without serious people driving it. The American working class is not dominated by meteors or deadbeats—at least not yet. There is cause for concern, but we have not collapsed as of today.

Make it your mission to expand the group of true professionals and shrink the outside groups. Hire, fire, and manage performance for this purpose. It's a full-time role to make sure your organization has the performing talent to realize your plan. Take it seriously. Meteors and deadbeats will hang around if you let them. Don't be accommodating.

If you own or belong to a larger organization, you will probably have to begin with some housecleaning in the legal and/or human resources departments. Many restraints to necessary management strategies originate in these groups. Clear your mind, gird for strength, and get on with it. In a competitive marketplace, it's change or die. You may as well go down fighting.

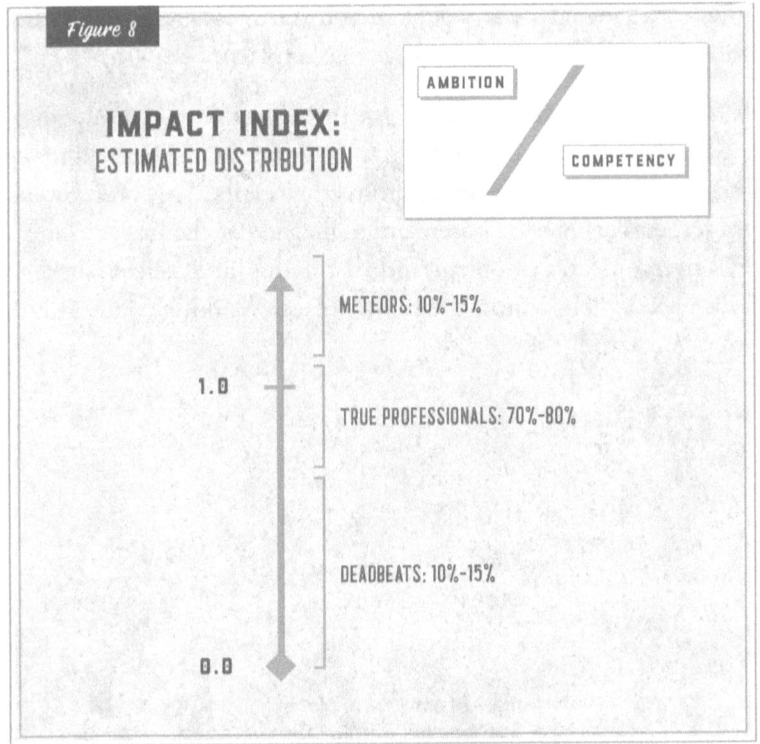

DISTRIBUTION OF THE WORKFORCE

Any organization that obsesses with the org. chart has lost its way. Defined roles can help us stay organized and avoid chaos, but what drives an organization is behavior. Boxes on the org. chart do not provide the readiness or ability to solve problems and can be detrimental to both. Life and business are all about solving problems, achieving goals. Focus on fundamental human behavior and you will have a successful team and organization. Right behavior gets things done. Everything else is a distraction.

Inherent human tendency is to associate with people who are like us. They look like us, think like us, have similar backgrounds, etc. We like a comfort factor. This is bad news in business. This inherent tendency creates gaps in your business competency that will be exploited in a competitive marketplace.

With the Impact Index, you go for the skills that you need, wherever you may find them, and you manage behaviors that will make these skills effective, therefore producing results. True professional team members, when chosen and managed per the Impact Index, will overcome any problem and distraction and deliver success. This means a big win in the marketplace, Working Man. This is what you want.

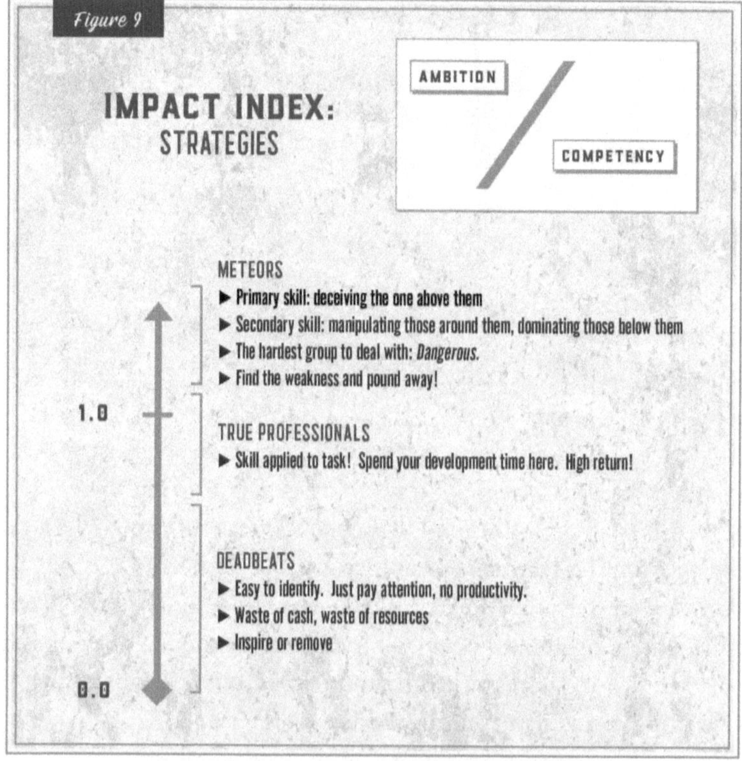

MANAGEMENT STRATEGIES USING THE IMPACT INDEX

Figure 9 is a shorthand reference to key management strategies for each group. Now, with these strategies in focus, we make it happen. We apply the concept. Accept the fact, like it or not, that these three groups exist in your workplace, within your company.

First comes assessment. What employees fit each group? As stated early in this chapter, this can be done formally or informally. "Formally" means to create tests and numerical measurements. The most practical approach, however, is to use the Impact Index informally. So, how does one create an assessment that can be applied with an informal measurement?

It is enabled and underpinned with a simple and effective process: observe and document behaviors. Pay attention to behaviors, which are the most important part of a team. It's what you should be doing anyway. Now, with the Impact Index, you have context, a tool to make these observations effective.

Write the observations down. Clear patterns amenable to coaching will become apparent. If you join this with standard empirical performance measurements associated with relevant tasks, you have a very powerful development framework.

For meteors, their primary skill is deceiving the manager or two above them. Their entire strategy is to conquer an organization to maximize pay and status. They don't intend to waste time on knowing what they are doing or speaking of. They simply want to advance as quickly as possible. Fooling the org. chart box they report to is paramount—the person or two they call boss cannot be allowed to know what they are up to. A meteor will be obsessed with relationship management up the chain of command.

Similarly, their secondary skill is manipulating those beside them, those at similar levels in the org chart, and dominating those below them. This secondary skill is meant to support the primary skill, by deceiving the one who grants promotions. They will often terrorize their underlings into submission and silence and hide nonperformance from peers to avoid bad feedback. They orchestrate a good assessment from their manager—without putting in the effort to do it the old-fashioned way, through hard work and results.

The meteors are a difficult group to deal with. They are very skilled and practiced at deception. This is a dangerous bunch. They threaten your organization. However, there is a key point to understand. By definition, a meteor has weaknesses. They have left behind true skill development, thinking that is beneath them. They are too clever for their own good. They believe shortcuts are the quicker path to success.

In so doing, they leave major gaps in their skill sets, and this is the key to finding them out and removing them. Observe carefully, find the weakness, and pound away! Gear discussions and performance reviews to these weaknesses. Remember, you need documented, specific examples. Bear down on these themes and discoveries, with no mercy.

With this managerial approach, you will get critical information in return. The meteor may turn out to prove you wrong. If this is true, the employee, when under scrutiny, will respond by developing and/or displaying skill, which will tell you that maybe you misread the person. You then adjust accordingly. If a suspected meteor, through behavior and demonstrated results, proves you wrong, then reclassify.

If, however, you are right, and this employee is truly a meteor, their response will tell you everything you need to know. You will see more deception, ever-deeper deceit, and no evidence of skill or true productivity. There will very likely be further acts of misbehavior, all of which will give you the facts you need to terminate employment.

It can take some time to uncover a meteor. They are good at what they do, but what they do never serves your organization well.

Take the time necessary, uncover behaviors, and manage them out. You owe it to the true professionals on the team. They expect you to do your job. Don't disappoint them.

There is nothing more discouraging for true professionals on a team than to see meteors or deadbeats elevated by management. It is a morale and productivity killer. The true professional will lose faith in you as an owner or manager. They will no longer believe that you know what you are doing or that you care about success. And they will leave. You will be taking your organization in the exact wrong direction.

There is a critical need for you as a supervisor to carefully manage this behavior in your direct reports. If you don't, you are leaving an incredibly difficult task for others to handle, while the meteor's behaviors continue to threaten your business plan. And the threat grows with time. As meteors succeed, they are emboldened. When promoted, they are worse than ever. As they grow bolder, the stakes get higher. A crash is coming, and management neglect only increases the collateral damage.

Managing a meteor when you are their supervisor is difficult, but it is a monumental task to manage a meteor who is your peer or your boss. Every time you encounter a meteor, that person has people around them as working peers, as colleagues. Much of the time, they also have people under them as direct reports.

As a peer and especially as a direct report, dealing with a meteor requires a great deal of courage. You must have a clear mind, hard facts at your disposal, and a backbone of pure steel. You may get lucky, and someone up the chain catches on to what you are up against. Many times, though, you are on your own.

You have a difficult choice to make. You can flake out and do nothing. You can join the meteor in their behavior. Or you can serve the organization with integrity and take them on, which is what you said you would do when you joined.

You see, there is a foundation underneath the Impact Index, a layer upon which it rests: character. The entire idea rests upon integrity. The very first step to implementing the Index is getting honest with yourself. What can I actually do? What effort will it take to build the skills that I need for my goals? Am I willing to work that hard? Be honest, assess both thoroughly and accurately, and build from there.

Remember this tried-and-true axiom, Working Man—your ambition can take you places where your character cannot sustain you. You can dream your way straight into a disaster. Meteors have made this a full-time occupation.

A meteor is a person who is fundamentally dishonest. When challenging a meteor, you are first and foremost challenging their integrity, their character. Therefore, you have the difficult choice of how to proceed if this is a peer or supervisor. At worst, you could lose your job and income.

I encourage you to see the bigger picture. If your organization creates an environment where meteors are allowed to flourish, you don't want to be there anyway. If you created such an organization, shame on you. Be wise, be thorough, and be of good courage. Commit yourself to living and managing by the Impact Index. You and all around you will be better served. Be willing to manage with integrity within your organization, even if you are not the direct authority. It's a high calling, above and beyond. It's also the right thing to do.

Deadbeats are much easier to spot than meteors. Simply pay attention to their productivity. There will be none. Deadbeats are a waste of cash and resources. Observe and document facts regarding productivity, and then either inspire the deadbeats or remove them.

With a deadbeat, it should take no longer than 30–60 days to bring about change, including employment termination. Address the lack of productivity quickly, based on the facts, and give two to four weeks for a response. If the employee responds properly, you have gained another true professional. If not, cut your losses and move on.

The time required to deal with a meteor can vary greatly, almost always taking longer than identifying a deadbeat. Their ability to deceive slows discovery. But be relentless and undeterred. Your organization, your business plan, is at risk. Stay on point.

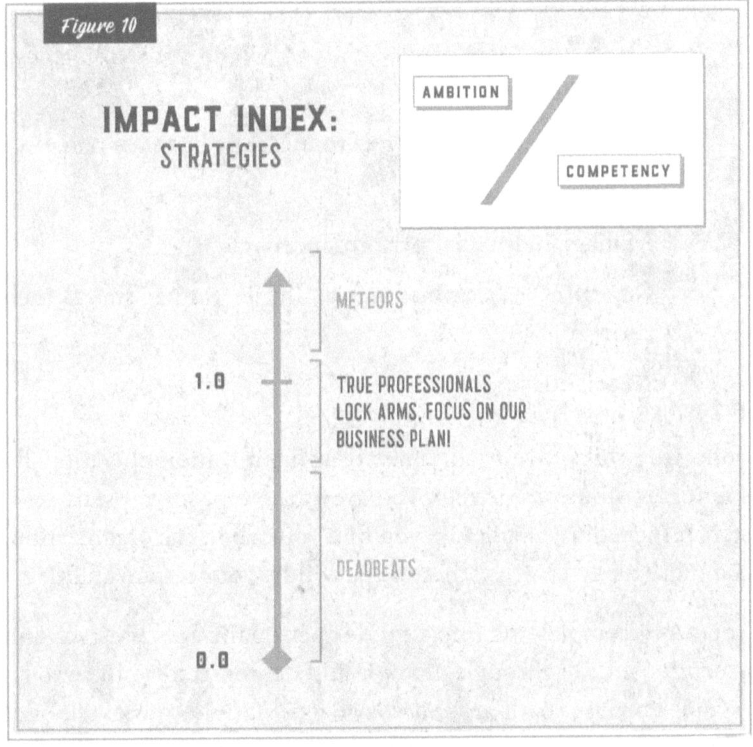

THE GOAL

Figure 10 above shows the goal for any organization, what every owner and manager should strive for. You want meteors and deadbeats to fade away. You want them to find a difficult existence in your group. Orchestrate it that way. Make it hard on them, and manage them out. You want an organization filled with true professionals! Make this crew happy, incent them, and work alongside them. First, be one yourself. Be an example. Then manage others by the same standard that you live and work by.

Here are the basic management steps that every business owner and supervisor must follow and master:

1. Set the business objective.

2. Set the business plan (details by which you will achieve the objective).

3. Identify required skill sets to meet the business plan.

4. Hire to these skill sets.

5. Manage individual performance.

6. Repeat at least annually, usually starting at step 2 each time.

7. Be relentless.

Following this process will make your organization operationally sound. As a business owner, you are at the top, so you start with step 1. Indeed, the higher up you find yourself in the organization, the more likely it is that these steps will be your responsibilities.

You should employ the Impact Index personally at every step—no exceptions. Lead through example and demonstrate your seriousness of purpose to all around you, particularly to those who will work under you. They deserve your best. Dream big and develop the skills to match the dream. After tending to yourself, the entire point of management is to create a business objective and plan, then create a workforce of true professionals focused on a common goal. Rest assured, true professionals will lock arms and get it done!

EXAMPLES FROM PERSONAL EXPERIENCE

I want to help you out even more, Working Man. I've had a full career to practice this method. There's no point in withholding experiential knowledge. Find below some personal encounters with deadbeats and meteors. To protect privacy, I won't divulge names or key details, but everything you read here is factual, a part of history. Hopefully, this will help you understand and apply the Impact Index technique as you build your own career. And, as a cherry on top, I think you will find it entertaining.

Meteors

These are the toughest, Working Man, so let's start here. This example will show how critical it is to identify and take action with a meteor and what it takes to follow through.

This event happened late in my career. I was serving on the executive team of a growing, midsize company. Our executive team had successfully created and executed business plans for several years. Our track record was very good. A key department-head job position came open, and we filled the job with all diligence. We were all closely involved in the recruitment.

The position was a direct report to my friend and colleague on the executive team, but the position supported all of us—a cross-team reporting arrangement. I was responsible for all of operations, and my interaction with this position was extensive. The cross-team arrangement made interactions complex, but this is normal in a teamwork environment. And there was no other practical way to set the organization. Ultimately, you put the org. chart aside and focus on getting the job done.

Our business was consumer retail in nature with an extensive field/community employee presence. Our products also had strong seasonal components, which meant that a significant portion of our revenue and profit growth came at key times of the year.

After a few months on the job for this department head, I began getting reports from field staff about the department head being difficult to work with. This was odd, because interactions between this person, me, and the executive team were flawless. We were all impressed.

Nonetheless, even with our confidence in this department head and lack of personal confirmation and shared experience for these complaints, I followed up. I was an experienced and committed practitioner of the Impact Index at this point, and I investigated with diligence. Most importantly, I wrote things down. I spoke with appropriate staff at all levels and documented what I found.

This management work took several weeks, a handful of months, and then came a turning point. We were entering one of our key seasonal-growth periods. It was early, just a couple of weeks in, and I noticed we were missing fundamental business goal metrics. We were missing our growth-plan targets.

I went into action immediately. I narrowed down the problem to a key region, and I went on the road. I put over a thousand miles on a company vehicle to track things down. I interviewed field staff in our branches and found what had happened.

This department head, whom we had trusted, single-handedly and independently decided to change certain company policies. The changes had a significant, negative impact on business growth. I was livid.

First things first, we corrected the policy changes within hours. Communications and field follow-up were put in place straight-away. Business growth trends were corrected, but that early miss carried through the year. The trend line for revenue was corrected, but the damage could not be overcome, and we ended the year short of our plan targets.

Next came dealing with the department head. I pulled the employee into my office and addressed their behavior in the most direct terms. Out of that conversation, and many closely sequenced follow-ups, came a world of information. I had every fact and piece of evidence I needed. Actions and motivations were all laid bare.

We had hired a meteor. I will call this one Department Meteor. Department Meteor had fooled every single one of us. In my response to complaints and employee actions, I followed the strategy stated earlier for breaking down meteors. I found the weakness, homed in, and pounded away. This broke the dam of deception and gave us everything we needed to correct our mistake.

Termination of employment was the outcome, but the damage had been done. We suffered disgruntled employees, disruption of business operations, and a missed annual business plan. However, it would have been much worse without a framework to deal with this meteor. The framework shortened the cycle times and directed our actions.

The documentation I created along the way was critical, and I would emphasize this to all of you building a career in this teamwork-dominated workplace. Document. Write things down. You will need it.

Ideally, we would have screened out Department Meteor in the interviews and never hired the troublemaker in the first place. But this isn't realistic. We did things right in the hiring process—extensive interviews, skill assessment, background checks, reference checks. All the proper steps were taken. Meteors are just really good at fooling you. Deception is their primary skill. They build their career around it.

Do your best in the hiring process, but there is no substitute for diligent personnel management using the Impact Index. Listen to colleagues at all levels. Observe behavior. Document and have direct conversations for follow-up. As you see a weakness, drive it home. Give no room for evasion. The meteor will crack up and disintegrate before your very eyes. Department Meteor burned up fast upon determined and informed confrontation.

Working Man, if you are going to supervise staff, make up your mind now to have the courage and the plan to do what is right for the people you work with. Your company and your goals depend on you.

I will give a second example from personal experience in dealing with meteors. This one is the most difficult type of all—a meteor as a supervisor. This one brings a strain, Working Man. It is truly a difficult experience.

I wasn't green in my career, but I wasn't as seasoned as I needed to be either. I was about to get that way.

The role I carried at the time was leading a team with sizable profit and loss responsibilities. Key parts of the business plan were ours to deliver. I loved the job. It was right up my alley.

Problems with my supervisor showed up within days. I will call the supervisor Boss Meteor. The first sign was constant manipulation. This was the hallmark trait in all relationships with this individual, in all directions. Up, down, sideways, everything was spun to establish control. Honesty was dismissed as outdated and unrealistic for a competitive workplace. Nothing was straightforward, nothing was as it seemed, and a hidden agenda lay behind every word.

As time wore on, Boss Meteor upped the intensity and made their objective clear: absolute control and domination. Threats of all kinds were made at every opportunity—some overt, some latent, some subtle, but all with the same point. You either supported Boss Meteor's way at all times or your career was toast.

In Boss Meteor's mind, this provided their best chance at surviving and being promoted within the organization. All personnel and business relationships involved were merely tools, pawns to be used. Along the way, I realized I had to choose between integrity and professionalism—doing my job or keeping Boss Meteor happy. The two endpoints were no longer jointly achievable. In fact, they were opposing objectives, with no overlap involved.

This was a tough choice. My job and income were on the line; my family's financial stability was at risk. And you never know how job loss will affect your career. There was plenty of uncertainty involved. I was also more than a little angry at the organization for leaving me hanging out to dry. There was no help in dealing with Boss Meteor. I was on my own.

I talked a lot with my wife. Fortunately, we had built the type of marriage discussed in Chapters 3 and 4. And we needed it. I could not have survived without her.

With her full support, I fell back on the values I had been taught as a child, the values I accepted as my own through adulthood. As stated in Chapter 1, honesty was a key principle taught by my parents. Through the trials handed out by Boss Meteor, I could hear the words of my father ring in my ears. I can hear them still, even as I type them on this keyboard.

"Son, always tell the truth, no matter what it costs you."

Pop, I kept that precept. I did what you taught me to do.

After making my internal choice, I just did my job. I did it right, as it should be done. I treated my colleagues and employees well and my boss in a normal fashion. I was a true professional.

And Boss Meteor popped a bolt over it. Boss Meteor had lost me, and knew it, and went into hyperdrive. The manipulating stunts and tricks became more intense and ridiculous than ever, and I didn't care. I had made my choice. I would stick with deeper values. I would not make my money playing such games.

Then came the circumstance that would blow everything wide open. You see, Working Man, the marketplace does not care about the trickeries that might be happening within a particular company. This is why meteors are such a threat to your organization. Their stunts weaken your ability to deliver. The real boss, your customers, don't give a rat's behind about what org. chart games you are playing. They want a quality product at a competitive price. They want value.

Meteors kneecap your organization. All the time spent dealing with their rubbish is time that your competitors are using to beat you at attracting customers. And that happened to us, in a fatal way.

We got into serious pressure with a business plan involving a major product launch. Boss Meteor didn't notice that the games being played, games initiated at their own hand, were not up to the challenge. Key parts of the product launch were fabricated, made up. They were lies, plain and simple. Incompetence settled in to match the dishonesty, and our fate was sealed. Arrogance and incompetence are lethal pairings.

I can honestly say that I did my best to make up for Boss Meteor's failings. I influenced and changed everything I could and made Boss Meteor very upset in the process. But there was only so much

I could do. It wasn't enough. The cost to the company from this failed product launch was well north of $500 million. Ouch. And the fallout was severe.

Fortunately for me, my departure from the company came in such a way as to separate me from association with this disaster. It worked out in the end, although I couldn't really see that at the time. There was plenty of faith involved.

As I look back, I had an opportunity at a couple of points to stand up publicly, expose the fiasco, and resign. I didn't, and I wish I had. That is where my greenness came in. I didn't have the perspective of experience, the seasoning, to know for sure that it was the right thing to do.

I do now. And I tell you with firm conviction, Working Man, if you find yourself under the next Boss Meteor, steel yourself, gather your wits, make sure Working Woman is in support, and take that fool on. Your company and business plan are shot to hell anyway. You may as well keep your integrity and do what is right. Be a true professional, even when it is not easy, even at personal cost.

There is also a lesson here worth pointing out, Working Man. As mentioned briefly above, meteors believe the competition that really matters is between colleagues within a company. Catching that next rung on the corporate ladder, or whatever form of personal advancement a meteor has in mind, is all they care about. This is delusional, a falsity. The only competition that matters is happening outside the company—the competition for customers. Your colleagues are precious resources, helping you achieve a goal. Treat them as such.

As you develop in your career, Working Man, and leadership roles come your way, focus on this point. Make it explicit in how you manage yourself and employees. Your competition is outside the company, not within. Within the company should only be teamwork. Any other focus is foolish, which is the ultimate downfall of every meteor. In the end, a meteor is a fool.

The next Ken Lay, the wannabe Dennis Kozlowski, the next meteor—they are already in the workforce. They are working alongside colleagues as we speak. Who will notice? Who will take a stand?

Do yourself, your friends, your family, your community, and your nation a favor. Call these fools out. Get in their way. Make their lives difficult. Your life and legacy will be better served if you do.

Dead beats

One more example, Working Man—this one for a deadbeat. Through some organizational realignment, I inherited a team of highly educated and trained employees. There were quite a few of them, all possessing skills I was very familiar with. I knew their work and responsibilities well. I was in a strong position to take over personnel management.

One of these employees—I will call him Junior Deadbeat—had a very strange idea regarding public companies. Junior Deadbeat thought a publicly traded, for-profit company was like a library or national park. It belonged to the public; therefore, no real accountability existed. Supervisors could not enforce work standards or goals because it all belonged to the public.

I know this is hard to believe, but I gained the knowledge of Junior Deadbeat's belief through personal conversation. I heard it with my own ears.

And Junior Deadbeat was true to those beliefs. Junior conformed to no standard whatsoever. Productivity was strictly at their preference, which meant not much and not very often. And they did not count on the fact that their boss, me, would not tolerate such waste and negligence.

I went into full documentation mode and full performance-management mode. I assigned many tasks, had many conversations, and detailed everything in a performance log, all with Junior Deadbeat's name on it. Then, after gathering sufficient evidence, I fired Junior. Good riddance.

Now for the fun part. Junior Deadbeat happened to be of international origin, born outside the U.S., and Junior saw a legal opportunity. He gathered a team of likeminded lawyers and filed suit for unlawful termination. Junior and team played the race angle and thought hefty compensation was in order. The number they claimed was deep into nine figures—a lot of money.

During the deposition, Junior's lawyers were an imposing lot, obnoxious from the start. At one point, they dropped a document in front of me and asked if I recognized it. I replied, "Yes, I do. It is my document. I wrote it." The lawyers smiled. They thought they had me.

I proceeded to clean their clocks for about four hours. You see, Working Man, they had produced the performance log that I had written covering Junior Deadbeat's behavior. I had everything in writing, in black and white. Junior didn't have his document, just mine.

Junior's lawyers thought they could intimidate and manipulate me into their narrative. They had underestimated their opponent. I had them frustrated to no end by the time we wrapped up. At one point, Junior's lead lawyer stood over me, yelling in full voice about contempt, court sanctions, and all manner of punitive actions. I looked him straight in the eye, smiled, chuckled, and went back to work. I described Junior for what he was, a deadbeat. The truth is interesting that way—it is a rock upon which to stand.

The deposition lasted a total of 11 grueling, tension-filled hours. But I was ready. My prior diligence had me prepared. The case went deep into the court system and required a full six years to settle. We won. And the document I had prepared was the key evidence upon which the judge finally ruled.

During the deposition, while Junior's legal team was trying to play entrapment, I would often use the phrase "in my judgment as the managing supervisor." I noticed whenever I said that, Junior's lawyers would darken their demeanor and move on. So, I said it a lot. They knew what that would mean in the court record and how a judge would weigh it. It doomed their case. Everything I wrote and said was the truth, and because it was written down, Junior's team had a tough time manipulating it.

I hope you find these examples illuminating, Working Man. I provide them for your benefit. You will have your own. Use the Impact Index, and your company and career will be well served.

KEYS TO NAVIGATING THE MODERN BUSINESS ENVIRONMENT

Along with the Impact Index, Working Man, here are key points that will bring you purpose and success in this modern business environment in which we make a living. Take these one at a time, ponder their meaning for your particular circumstance, and they should inspire you to positive action.

- Talents are God's gift individually wrapped in that flesh and blood package you call home, a body. God's calling rests squarely upon the way you are made. It's not a dark mystery, although it does require discovery. What are your talents? How did God make you? God leaves no one out. Everyone is blessed with a set of talents. Find them, apply them, and develop them into skills.

- Having discovered these talents, which will also be what you enjoy (God is gracious, generous, kind, and favorable in that way), develop the highest level of skill that you possibly can based on these talents. For some, this means a GED high school equivalent. For others, it means cross-training in the workplace. It could mean graduate school, medical school, law school, or advanced professional education. Some will be best served by the vocational degree path. It might mean several of those things. Figure it out and have a blast doing so. This is a life of faith and a life well lived. Live with purpose in your career. Make it a path of discovery, beginning with the way God made you.

- Rest squarely on the Impact Index. Practice it every day.

- Develop and live out the character traits necessary to make the Impact Index possible. You can never be a true professional without deep character and integrity. Be honest. Everything else is a sham.

- Develop soft skills: social skills, communication skills (written and verbal), the ability to interact with individuals and groups, the ability to connect on a personal level with others. If you stack these soft skills on top of compelling technical expertise, you have a recipe for success.

- This will be a very powerful package in the workplace. Investment capital in this modern economy is looking for a return and craves leadership of this quality and type. Leadership roles will fall to someone who can create a plan producing said return and can also lead people to execute that plan. There are vast, diverse, and growing opportunities down this path. Knock yourself out!

Once again, there you have it, Working Man. A frame has been created and complexity has been conquered. The challenge of productivity in the modern workplace can be handled, not with ease but with confidence and to high effect. Go forth, and make money!

Chapter 7

POLITICS AND ECONOMICS: THE MORAL VIEW (YES, THERE IS SUCH A THING)

WE'VE BEEN TAKING on big ideas, Working Man, big problems of amazing complexity at first glance. Let's not stop now. Here's another, national in scope, and it matters to your daily life. My goal in this conversation is to cover the critical items that matter to your daily habits and lifetime goals, and this one is on the list in a big way.

In my view, the national debt is the largest and most imminent threat facing the American citizen today. It's worse than China, worse than Islamic jihad, and far worse than Russia. It's a seismic problem—and it's not an accident. The threat exists due to deliberate choice. It has been created intentionally, and we will have to deal with it the same way—intentionally.

As mentioned in the Introduction, we have been trying to avoid the topic for as long as possible. If we don't talk about it, it will go away, right? Unfortunately, that is not the case. A lot of people in powerful places have a vested interest in you not noticing, or caring, about the effects of excessive national indebtedness. They work hard at keeping you distracted.

I'm going to speak straight to you—no deception, no tricks. And, on top of that, I will keep the method we've had from the beginning of this discussion—look for themes, foundational principles, bedrock. We'll look deep for the things that matter.

Those that want you distracted make a lot of noise about a lot of things that are not important, oftentimes not even related. And that is the point—talk about something, anything, other than the national debt, because that involves the type of change the folks embedded in public places of power and influence don't want.

A common deflection is to say that the United States has always had debt, that this is nothing new. In a strict sense, this statement is true, but it's highly misleading. We've never had this level of debt for the reasons we are incurring it (Appendix, Figure 14).[55] And don't listen to any reference to the national debt that doesn't include Social Security debt. That is pure deception. Leaving out Social Security can drop the percentage of federal debt to gross domestic product, or GDP, by as much as 30 points. Don't believe

---

[55] "Composition of Outlays: 1940–2029," Office of Management and Budget (OMB), The White House, Historical Tables, table 6.1, https://www.whitehouse.gov/omb/budget/historical-tables/.

it. The federal government is on the hook for that debt just like any other public debt. It must be paid, by law.

And, by the way, the best way to analyze the federal public debt is to look at a ratio of total debt to GDP. In other words, the level of public debt as a ratio to the size of the U.S. annual economy, ignoring international trade flows. We will use that measure here in our discussion.

Look at the current level of federal debt and what we are spending it on, Working Man, and notice some key facts. The last time we had federal debt anywhere near current levels of percentage to GDP was right after World War II (Appendix, Figure 15).[56] I don't think anyone would argue with that investment. The U.S. remained free, our constitutional government stayed intact, and we rid the world of tyrannical threats from Asia and Europe. That's pretty impressive.

And as we begin to highlight and break down the current predicament, Working Man, stop for a moment and look back. Look back in history and see what the United States has overcome as a nation. We beat the British Empire at the height of its power, not once but twice. We won both the American Revolution and the War of 1812. That alone is staggering.

We won not one but two World Wars. The entry of the United States into both World War I and World War II was decisive. We survived the Civil War, ending the tragic practice of slavery on U.S. soil. Countless tragedies and conflicts, large and small, across the American frontier defined us but did not end us. We won the Cold War, came through the Vietnam War and the Korean War, all major conflicts with all manner of debate and vitriol. We were only stronger at the end of it.

---

[56] "Federal Debt to GDP," Longtermtrends, accessed April 4, 2024, https://www.longtermtrends.net/us-debt-to-gdp/.

Through all of that, America has overcome and remains a beacon of freedom to the world. That is an extraordinary and inspiring history. What a story, what a tale we have to tell.

Is it possible, Working Man, after all that, that we go down over money? That should be unthinkable, impossible, inconceivable, beyond belief, and yet, here we are. We have a public crisis that demands attention. What will we do? Let's use our same method, our same approach to problem-solving. We break it down, frame it, and solve it one step at a time.

To understand current habits and attitudes, it's important to look at the bedrock of ideas regarding public expenditure and the role of the federal government in the U.S. economy. For that, you must look squarely at John Maynard Keynes.[57]

Keynes is one of the most famous economists to ever live. More than anyone, Keynes established and promoted the idea of government fiscal stimulus as the way to stabilize the economy. The term is prominent to this very day, thanks to Keynes.

His idea is straightforward, easy for all to understand. If the government spends money, it will provide financial, monetary stimulus to the economy, resulting in jobs and income wherever government projects are carried out. When a government project ensues, materials will be purchased, labor hired, and money spent. Regular American citizens benefit; therefore, government fiscal stimulus is a very good thing.

That sounds promising, right? Who could argue against that? Better still, forget the projects; just pay money directly to citizens. That's a surefire win, correct? Money goes straight to my pocket, and all is well.

---

[57] *Encyclopedia Britannica*, s.v. "John Maynard Keynes," last updated January 24, 2024, https://www.britannica.com/biography/John-Maynard-Keynes.

Do you have a financial problem? Here's a government check. Have you suffered a setback or two? Here's a government benefit. Do you think wealth is unfairly spread across the nation's citizens? Well, the just and mighty hand of government is right there for you. Problem solved.

As these fairy-tale promises sweep the country, capturing vote after vote, Working Man, take a deeper look. Look at foundational things, bedrock things. Let me help you with that.

If you want to stop a leftist in their tracks, if you wish to make them think about things they never expected you to understand, let alone mention, take a look at this. Go right to the source, to Keynesian theory. Keynes's equations are listed below, with an explanation following.

- AD (GNP) = C + I + G + (X − M)[58]

- Where

    o   AD = aggregate demand = gross national product

    o   C = Y − T

        ▪   C = consumption

        ▪   Y = income

        ▪   T = taxes

---

[58]   John M. Keynes, *The General Theory of Employment, Interest and Money* (New York: Harcourt, Brace and Company, Inc., 1936), Book III;
William H. Branson, *Macroeconomic Theory and Policy*, 3rd ed. (New York: Harper and Row Publishers, 1989);
Bill Gibson, "Check Your Understanding: The Keynesian Model," The University of Vermont, June 4, 2017, https://www.uvm.edu/~wgibson/CYU/CYU_Keynesian_model.pdf;
Rudlger Dornbusch and Stanley Fischer, *Macroeconomics*, 5th ed. (New York: McGraw-Hill Publishing Company, 1990);
David J. Ott, Attiat F. Ott, and Jang H. Yoo, *Macroeconomic Theory* (Lanham, MD: University Press of America, 1983).

- o I = investment

- o G = government spending

- o X = exports

- o M = imports

Ignoring international trade flows, we have gross domestic product, or

- AD (GDP) = C + I + G, with C, I, and G defined as above.

A lot of fancy math can follow these equations.[59] Massive amounts of academic prowess have been involved in creating this fancy math. But it isn't necessary to get the main points. Any grade-schooler with simple addition and subtraction skills can comprehend it.

Let's take the clear route, Working Man, and leave the fancy math to others. The Keynes argument, simply stated and continuing to this day, is this: You see that *G* in the GDP equation? If government spends more, the economy (GDP) is larger. If government spends less, the economy is smaller. Therefore, Working Man, if you want a larger economy, increase government spending. This is called government fiscal stimulus.

Anyone should be able to understand that, right? Ahh, the power of simple suggestion, Working Man. It can take you far, but will it take you to the finish line? Can it deliver on big promises?

---

[59] Karl Whelan, "The Modern New-Keynesian Model," School of Economics, University College Dublin, Spring 2016, https://www.karlwhelan.com/MAMacro/part9.pdf;
Guillermo A. Calvo, "Staggered Prices in a Utility-Maximizing Framework," *Journal of Monetary Economics* 12, no. 3 (September 1983): 383–98, https://doi.org/10.1016/0304-3932(83)90060-0;
Ben J. Heijdra, *Foundations of Modern Macroeconomics,* 3rd ed. (Oxford: Oxford University Press, 2017).

The problem with the government fiscal stimulus promise is that it is a myth. It is not true. All you need to prove this is the very equations that Keynes himself used. Look just a bit more closely at these same equations. Again, nothing fancy. Just simple math—addition and subtraction.

Stare at the equation, and you will see two obvious and fatal problems to a nonetheless almost immortal fallacy:

1. These are only accounting equations that do not incorporate the most fundamental aspect of economics: individual choice, both consumer and producer. Accounting equations can only be descriptive in nature.

   Fatal flaw 1: Keynesian economics is not a theory of economic behavior. At most, it is a descriptive tool and an insidiously deceptive tool at that.

Working Man, if you've been a diehard, committed leftist, or are at least open to the idea, I hate to bust your dreams wide open, but Keynes's equations don't support the promises. They have nothing to do with choice, only what has been chosen. You can cut some fancy graphs, that's for sure, but they are unrelated to how citizens' lives may be affected by a government policy, because individual choice is not allowed in the equations of Keynes. Consumer choice has already happened.

If you want to see choice properly included in a real economic theory, look at the theory of consumer demand and the theory of producer supply, known jointly as microeconomic theory.[60] I won't cover these in detail in this book, but I can assure you that choice is baked into the equations. Individual choice is intrinsic and foundational. You get no such thing with Keynes.

2. At some point, the discussion around government stimulus must answer a basic question. The discussion can be very technical and sophisticated (e.g., rational expectations[61]), or one can make the same point by simply staring at the Keynes equation and asking a simple question: "What if you set G = T?"

    Fatal Flaw 2: Government stimulus is a myth. Government spending must be paid for, dollar for dollar, through a reduction, either now or later, of aggregate demand via taxes. If a populace is foolish enough to set G > T and believe the lie of government stimulus, then you can add interest expense to the bill. T is now higher, and the full bill comes due, guaranteed.

---

[60] Jonathan Levin and Paul Milgrom, *Consumer Theory* (Stanford University, 2004), https://web.stanford.edu/~jdlevin/Econ%20202/Consumer%20Theory.pdf;
Jonathan Levin and Paul Milgrom, *Producer Theory* (Stanford University, 2004), https://web.stanford.edu/~jdlevin/Econ%20202/Producer%20Theory.pdf;
James M. Henderson and Richard E. Quandt, *Microeconomic Theory: A Mathematical Approach,* 3rd ed. (New York: McGraw-Hill Book Company, 1980);
Edgar K. Browning and Jacquelene M. Browning, *Microeconomic Theory and Applications,* 3rd ed. (Northbrook, IL: Scott, Foresman and Company, 1989);
Alpha C. Chiang, *Fundamental Methods of Mathematical Economics,* 3rd ed. (New York: McGraw-Hill Book Company, 1984);
Hal R. Varian, *Microeconomic Analysis,* 3rd ed. (New York: W.W. Norton & Company, 1992).
[61] John F. Muth, "Rational Expectations and the Theory of Price Movements," *Econometrica* 29, no. 3 (1961): 315–335;
Carla Tardi, "Rational Expectations Theory Definition and How It Works," Investopedia, last modified September 19, 2023, https://www.investopedia.com/terms/r/rationaltheoryofexpectations.asp;
Robert E. Lucas, Jr. and Thomas J. Sargent, eds., *Rational Expectations and Econometric Practice*, vol. 1, (Minneapolis, MN: The University of Minnesota Press, 1981), http://www.jstor.org/stable/10.5749/j.ctttssh5.

We can make this even easier, Working Man. Let's substitute terms in the equation above and simplify. We get this:

- $AD (GDP) = Y - T + I + G$

Just stare right at it, and ask the question again. What if you set $G = T$? The vaunted, all-powerful government stimulus, the savior of mankind, is a big fat zero.

That fact is hard on a leftist. It's hard to accept that you've believed a lie and foisted that same lie on others. Especially if you are getting paid based on the lie or if you are paid to keep lying. Try having this conversation with a federal bureaucrat. They won't be calm.

Working Man, if you go back to foundational principles, bedrock ideas, here is where you stand: Keynesian theory debunks itself, right in front of the reader, plain to see. All one can say in the face of this glaring fact is that folks believed, and continue to believe, in the fallacy of government stimulus because they wish to. It is a religion.

If we want to believe something bad enough, we will risk a great deal living as though it is true. Due to deficit spending, the American economy is currently on the roulette table. We are risking a great deal to continue believing the Keynesian hoax.

And here's a word to the wise on evaluating economic theories, or any theory, for that matter: If a proposed theory won't survive grade-school math and logic, turn your back and walk away. Keynes's theory fails the test.

Leftists possess a burning passion and desire to view the American economy as a monolith. I think many of us know why: monoliths can be controlled. This is an error shot through with malice, an error leading always and forever to the same destination—a monolithic mistake.

You see, Working Man, the U.S. economy is not a monolith. It is built from the bottom up, not the top down. It exists one transaction, one decision, one consumer, and one producer at a time. There is no "system," a word leftists love. There are only choices.

The only correct and proper way to view a nation's economy is as a summation of individuals and individual markets. Just because you sum them up doesn't change what they are—individuals making choices, pursuing what they believe to be best.

You might look at that fact and say, "That's incredibly complex. How could you ever formulate a national policy in that framework?" And you would be exactly right. Now, you are catching on. Humility is in order, and severe restraint, when considering national economic policy.

How could a federal bureaucrat, a technocratic, self-proclaimed "expert," possibly know better than folks on the ground making things work? The truth is, they don't, but they are ever confident and forceful—never more so than when they err.

I think it is worth noting that John M. Keynes was never trained in economics. He was a trained mathematician, a very gifted one, with a strong interest in philosophy, probability, politics, and economics.[62] He was a talented, exceptionally accomplished, and influential man. He also overreached and should stand corrected in his error. His faulty economic theories have caused a great deal of damage. It's past time to move on and avail ourselves of a better way.

Sometimes timing is everything. Keynes offered his theories while the world suffered the throes of the Great Depression, while at the same time—a fact of great significance—he addressed a void in

---

[62] *Encyclopedia of Mathematics*, s.v. "Keynes, John Maynard," last updated March 21, 2023, http://encyclopediaofmath.org/index.php?title=Keynes,_John_Maynard&oldid=53062.

economic theory, that of macroeconomic theory. Keynes was the first to offer a comprehensive view of an economy, a top-down view of a nation's wealth with an analytical base, not solely conceptual, something revolutionary at the time. There is no economic text more famous than his *The General Theory of Employment, Interest, and Money.*

These two circumstantial facts, timing and being first on the scene, in my view, go a long way to explaining the revered and hallowed status many ascribe to Keynesian theory. In the 1930s, there was a deep well of public sentiment for government "to do something." Keynes met that desire with full academic credo and cover. Kudos to Mr. Keynes for his great accomplishment. He was also wrong; let's not forget that.[63]

Then, of course, alongside Keynes we have the Austrian school of economic thought, a contrasting and far-superior alternative.[64] F. A. Hayek, Ludwig Von Mises, Milton Friedman, and many other proponents. The two fatal errors of Keynes have been corrected. Individual consumer and producer choice, the bedrock of any economy, is intrinsic and paramount, as they must be in any economic theory or assessment. And there is no hand-waving when it comes to government spending and taxation.

Better economic theories, with better subsequent policies and outcomes, are current and available. Choice is at the heart of daily living, and therefore choice is the centerpiece of economics. Theories and following policies must feature and have as their architecture the very same: individual choice.

---

63 Lucas and Sargent, "After Keynesian Macroeconomics," in *Rational Expectations and Econometric Practice*, vol. 1, 295–320.

64 Steven Horwitz, "Austrian Economics: The Next Generation," in *Advances in Austrian Economics*, vol. 23, 1ˢᵗ ed. (Leeds: Emerald Publishing, 2019).

WHY YOU SHOULD CARE

The theory and implications are clear, Working Man, but why should you care? Why should it matter? Why do we need to get political? All was going well with this discussion, and then we bring politics into it. Is that really necessary?

You have a good point. Politics is a mess of a topic and not where you normally take a friendly conversation. I would not do it unless it mattered. I wouldn't waste your time.

You see, the national debt is one of those things that doesn't matter a single bit, until it matters, and then it matters a lot. As in, when launched, it saturates everything in sight with a negative effect. We don't have to take that risk. It's completely unnecessary and very unwise.

We could be here a very long time discussing all aspects and implications of excessive national debt, but we won't. We will cover only a very short list. You don't need a long list to understand how this affects your daily life, Working Man, how it affects the legacy you are trying to build. That's why we started this conversation, and we will stick to the point.

Remember this about politics, Working Man—the only thing that matters in politics is policy. Everything else is theater. We will hit key policy ideas related to the national debt, and that is enough. Those are what matter. They affect your daily work and what you strive to leave behind.

First of all, Working Man, as disgusting, frustrating, and boring as politics can be, there is one fact you cannot escape. You must have a valid currency. You need a medium that facilitates transactions. You need to buy, sell, and trade. Bartering is a good thing, dealing in goods and services only, but you can go only so far with that. How many goats do you really want to keep around for trade, Working Man? I think you see what I mean.

Without a valid, sound, stable currency, a national economy is going nowhere. Your financial well-being, and general well-being, depend on it. It's a must have. It is basic infrastructure that any modern government should provide.

There is a bare minimum of two things that a national currency must maintain to have validity:

1. It must be difficult to counterfeit to maintain legitimacy.

2. It must maintain stable value, or stable purchasing power, over time.

A combination of the U.S. Secret Service (investigations) and the Department of the Treasury (development and printing of counterfeit-proof currency) through the U.S. Mint are purposed with the mission of taking care of item 1. I must admit—and I'm not easy on federal agencies—they do a solid job. Our counterfeit problems with the U.S. dollar are admirably low.[65]

On item 2, stable value, or stable purchasing power, over time, our track record is not so impressive. We are struggling with this one. A number of things can go wrong here, all of them policy related. Let's focus on just two things.

Types and Effects of Inflation

We've just had a bout with inflation, from 2021 to early 2024 and counting, as of this writing. Nobody in this country has been helped by this latest run-in with spiraling prices.

---

[65] Ruth Judson and Richard Porter, "Estimating the Worldwide Volume of Counterfeit U.S. Currency: Data and Extrapolation," Division of Monetary Affairs, Board of Governors of the Federal Reserve System, September 2003, https://www.federalreserve.gov/pubs/feds/2003/200352/200352pap.pdf.

Working Man, what we have just experienced is known as aggregate demand inflation—in other words, price inflation caused by the aggregate demand of goods exceeding the aggregate supply. More goods, on a broad basis, are in demand than we have available for purchase. This means prices are going up. And boy, did they ever. Unless you've been living under a rock in recent times, you know all about it.

The cause of aggregate demand inflation can be complex, and of course politicians are ever so honest about their role in fouling things up, but the cause of inflation from 2021 to now is clear: excess government spending. This one is fiscal in cause, no doubt about it, and entirely avoidable.

What we have experienced recently is just a small taste of inflation and its effects. It can get much worse (Appendix, Figure 16).[66] The downgrade in purchasing power of the U.S. dollar is real, painful, and destructive. You see it every time you walk into a store to purchase staples. It wrecks your budget and your dreams in tandem. Inflation must be avoided. And it can be; it's a policy choice.

However, there is a second way inflation can downgrade the value of a currency. It is important to note that we have never seen this second inflationary cause in the U.S. It is common around the world and through history, but Americans have not yet indulged the beast of which we are about to speak. Count your lucky stars, Working Man, and enjoy the moment, because if we keep to the path we are on with the national debt, this ferocious beast will be our bedmate.

This second cause is best known as bond market inflation. Aggregate demand inflation is related to goods and services

---

[66] "Historical Inflation Rates: 1914–2024," US Inflation Calculator, CoinNews Media Group Company, https://www.usinflationcalculator.com/inflation/historical-inflation-rates/;
Michael Bryan, "The Great Inflation," Federal Reserve History, November 22, 2013, https://www.federalreservehistory.org/essays/great-inflation.

bought and sold within an economy. Bond market inflation is related to risk involved in the debt markets used to fund the national fiscal deficit—bonds and securities.

It's simple, Working Man. Every dollar the U.S. federal government borrows occurs via the feds selling bonds or securities to cover the cash flow need. The feds are on the hook to repay these using your money, of course, with interest. The buyers of these bonds and securities are commonly public institutions outside the U.S. government, both foreign and domestic, private and governmental. Some debt is held within our own government; most of it is not.[67]

These outside buyers have a certain expectation regarding the likelihood that the debt they have purchased will be paid back to them, with interest. Risk of payment default is a consideration in every purchase. As you would think, they expect repayment. Otherwise, they wouldn't purchase the debt.

And there's the catch, Working Man, the thing politicians and leftists don't like to talk about. If we start missing interest payments, or show any sign that we are anywhere near such status, the buyers will demand a higher interest rate on current and future debt purchases to account for the higher risk of nonpayment they face. And that's if they buy the debt at all.

This then forces increases in interest rates, wholly unrelated to aggregate demand, hence the name "bond market inflation." Interest rates are forced to rise due to the risk of the nation's economy not being able to pay back obligations incurred by its government.

---

[67] "Securities (B): Portfolio Holdings of U.S. and Foreign Securities, U.S. Department of the Treasury," U.S. Department of the Treasury, accessed March 3, 2024, https://home.treasury.gov/data/treasury-international-capital-tic-system-home-page/tic-forms-instructions/securities-b-portfolio-holdings-of-us-and-foreign-securities; "Which Countries Own the Most US Debt?," USA Facts, last modified October 4, 2023, https://usafacts.org/articles/which-countries-own-the-most-us-debt/.

Think it through, Working Man. If interest rates are rising due to risk of repayment failure, this increases the cost of the debt, increasing the amount of a debt payment, making it even more difficult to make a payment, which increases the risk of nonpayment, which increases the interest rate, which increases … And on it goes. We've entered a spiral of destruction.

This is a disaster. Aggregate demand inflation is child's play by comparison. There is a known cure for aggregate demand inflation: raise interest rates to the point of causing a recession, bringing prices back down and restoring productivity as the basis for the economy. It's painful, but it works. It's proven. This remedy pulled the United States out of the stagnant, inflationary cycle of the 1970s and into the long cycle of prosperity we experienced beginning in the early 1980s.[68]

Bond market inflation, however, is much worse in effect, and it is very difficult to bring down. This has ruined national currencies, brought down governments, destroyed entire economies, and created social mayhem.[69] It is a nasty beast.

Without question, the best cure for bond market inflation is prevention. Don't get into that mess to begin with. If you find yourself looking for a cure, you are already ruined.

We skirted the edge of this in 2023. Annual net interest expense on the federal debt rose to $659 billion as of September 30, the end of fiscal year 2023. That is up 39% over fiscal year 2022 and

---

[68] Laurence B. Siegel, "How Paul Volcker Saved Our Country," VettaFi Advisor Perspectives, February 4, 2019, https://www.advisorperspectives.com/articles/2019/02/04/how-paul-volcker-saved-our-country;
Marvin Goodfriend and Robert G. King, "The Incredible Volker Disinflation" (working paper, National Bureau of Economic Research, Cambridge, MA, 2005), https://doi.org/10.3386/w11562.

[69] *Encyclopedia Britannica*, s.v. "Weimar Republic," last modified February 16, 2024, https://www.britannica.com/place/Weimar-Republic.

fully twice the amount of interest paid in fiscal year 2020.[70] We currently spend more on interest against the national debt than we spend on national defense.[71]

It's not a stretch to say that we are borrowing money to pay interest on the national debt. The credit markets have noticed.[72] Every junior high school student and beyond knows that will not work. Except our politicians, of course—they think the current status is just fine. Personally, I think an old expression is in order: "We have painted ourselves into a corner."

Here's the point, Working Man. Aggregate demand inflation crushes your dreams. Bond market inflation wipes your dreams from the face of the earth, along with any hope or means of achieving them. Inflation, whatever its source, is your enemy. Treat it that way. You are never better off in an inflationary environment, and you could be sacrificed by it.

You must be able to afford your principles. What value is dreaming if you can't fund those dreams? What's the point of your beliefs if you can't put heft behind them? That's the design and purpose of America. Dream, believe, have convictions, have ideas, and then pour your life into them. To have that freedom, to realize that promise, you need a currency you can count on. Currency is a medium, a tool, which gets you where you want to go. That currency must be sound and of stable value.

---

[70] Tami Luhby, "Interest Payments on the Nation's Debt Are Soaring, Adding Pressure to Congress' Spending Battle," CNN, last modified November 16, 2023, https://www.cnn.com/2023/11/16/politics/interest-payments-federal-government-debt/index.html.

[71] "What Is the National Debt Costing Us?," Peter G. Peterson Foundation, February 9, 2024, https://www.pgpf.org/blog/2024/02/what-is-the-national-debt-costing-us.

[72] "Fitch Downgrades the United States' Long-Term Rating to 'AA+' from 'AAA'; Outlook Stable," Fitch Ratings, August 1, 2023, https://www.fitchratings.com/research/sovereigns/fitch-downgrades-united-states-long-term-ratings-to-aa-from-aaa-outlook-stable-01-08-2023.

Working Man, stop listening to lying, thieving politicians and leftists that tell you the national debt doesn't matter. As stated earlier, it doesn't matter until it matters, and then it matters until you can't see straight. It obliterates your dreams right in front of you.

And we are running this risk due to a debunked religion, a misplaced belief, an ill-formed idea, a hoax—the myth of government fiscal stimulus. It is past time to wise up, Working Man. You should be working on behalf of your dreams, your legacy, those around you that you love, not some fool bureaucrat, politician, or leftist who lies for a living and steals or wastes what rightfully belongs to you.

If you need history or broader world experience to prove the point, it's easy to find. Study the following:[73]

- Current-day Venezuela.[74] It persistently carries the lowest Moody's credit rating of C, showing little chance of repayment for principal or interest on government debt.

- The Weimar Republic of 1920s Germany.[75] A wheelbarrow full of currency was required to purchase a single newspaper.

- Ireland.[76] It had persistently high inflation over long time periods, since at least 1969, leading to severely deteriorating purchasing power.

---

[73] Rick Orford, "Worst Cases of Hyperinflation Through History," SoFi, November 14, 2022, https://www.sofi.com/learn/content/worst-cases-hyperinflation-history/; "Hyperinflation Throughout History: Examples and Impact," Investopedia, September 23, 2023, https://www.investopedia.com/ask/answers/061515/what-are-some-historic-examples-hyperinflation.asp.

[74] "Venezuela, Government of," Moody's, accessed March 3, 2024, https://www.moodys.com/credit-ratings/Venezuela-Government-of-credit-rating-800876.

[75] Fid Backhouse et al., s.v. "Hyperinflation in the Weimar Republic," *Encyclopedia Britannica*, last modified February 29, 2024, https://www.britannica.com/event/hyperinflation-in-the-Weimar-Republic.

[76] "Inflation Rates in Ireland," WorldData.info, accessed March 3, 2024, https://www.worlddata.info/europe/ireland/inflation-rates.php.

- Greece, October 1944–47.[77] Prices doubled every 4.3 days.

- Zimbabwe, 2007–09.[78] The peak monthly inflation rate in November 2008 was 2,600%.

- Yugoslavia, October 1994.[79] Prices doubled every 34 hours.

- Hungary, 1946.[80] Prices doubled every 15.6 hours.

- France, 1790s.[81] The cost of ink to print a note of currency exceeded the value of the note itself.

The cause of debilitating inflation runs the gamut. War, mismanagement, political upheaval, hyperspending—you name it. But the point that matters is not varied and cannot be displaced: avoid it. Don't go anywhere near it. Demand this of your elected politicians, Working Man. We must talk politics here because your legacy, your life's work, is at risk. You and Working Woman cannot achieve your dreams without it.

[77] Yannis M. Ioannides, *Economic Consequences of World War II for Greece* (Medford, MA: Tufts University, 2004), https://sites.tufts.edu/yioannides/files/2012/09/Talk-OXI-Day-MaliotisCenter-Oct31-20041.pdf.

[78] "Economic Crisis in Zimbabwe," Synergia Foundation, October 18, 2018, https://www.synergiafoundation.org/insights/analyses-assessments/economic-crisis-zimbabwe.

[79] Vladimir Gligorov, "Yugoslavia and Development: Benefit and Costs," Yu Historija, accessed March 3, 2024, https://yuhistorija.com/economy_txt01.html.

[80] William A. Bomberg and Gail E. Makinen, "The Hungarian Hyperinflation and Stabilization of 1945–1946," *Journal of Political Economy* 91, no. 5 (1983): 801–24, https://doi.org/10.1086/261182.

[81] Kate Steir, "Understanding Hyperinflation, From Revolutionary France to Zimbabwe," *Smithsonian Voices* (blog), Smithsonian Magazine, April 1, 2022, https://www.smithsonianmag.com/blogs/national-museum-american-history/2022/04/01/understanding-hyperinflation/;
Pamfili Antipa, "The Fiscal Roots of Hyperinflation: A Historical Perspective," Banque de France, September 15, 2023, https://www.banque-france.fr/en/publications-and-statistics/publications/fiscal-roots-hyperinflation-historical-perspective.

The Path to Prosperity

The gateway to prosperity is not wide and multitudinous, Working Man. That lying leftist that I keep referring to is also a master at hand-waving, an expert at deception. They would like you to think there are many ways to an elevated standard of living, most of them involving government largesse. They are wrong. There is only one way: gains in productivity. If productivity never increases, incomes remain the same, and you bear the inherent risk of living with no upside.

If you are cruising along with no income gains, you still face all the negatives this world offers—disease, death, wars, famine, drought, accident, injury, etc. America has enjoyed a steadily increasing standard of living for many generations. We must rethink current conditions if we wish to keep that trend.

Productivity gains are the only gateway to prosperity, and these gains can only happen in two ways, one gateway and two gatekeepers:

1. Finding better, cheaper ways to produce current goods and services

2. Discovering and creating new goods and services to produce and supply

Fortunately, Working Man, and a reason for great optimism, is that the path to prosperity gets very wide at this point. This is why freedom works. There are infinite ways to accomplish these two things. The only limit is the human mind.

The gate is narrow, and the gatekeepers are only two in number. This should inform every policy decision made. You should be very firm with your vote and your viewpoint on this one, Working Man. If we don't get the gate and gatekeepers right, we will suffer dearly. If we do get them right, subsequently, the sky is the limit on wealth creation. There is enough variety and potential to keep everyone busy and prosperous for as long as we need.

The best and most prominent measurement of standard of living, or quality of life, is inflation-adjusted annual or monthly household income. This is your purchasing power, Working Man. This fuels your dreams. Notice that qualifier, "inflation-adjusted." If inflation is not held in check, you can create and discover and improve until the cows come home. Ultimately, you are doomed. It is all for nothing (Appendix, Figures 17 and 18).[82]

This is why we should oppose with vigor the leftist political tropes and policies. Their priorities are upside down. The focus has to be on fostering an economy based on productivity gains and keeping inflation in check. The individuals, you and I, Working Man, will take care of the rest. Give us a stable currency, and we will innovate our way to whatever we want.

Lying and thieving leftists, pardon the redundancies, will talk endlessly about the collective. I will talk about you and me, the individual. That is where things get done, families are built, societies are made healthy, and prosperity is created.

PROPERTY RIGHTS AND INDUSTRY: MANKIND'S GREATEST HOPE

Working Man, we've covered thoroughly the Keynesian hoax of government stimulus, the resulting deficit spending and national

---

[82] Gloria Guzman and Melissa Kollar, "Table C-1: Historical Median Income Using Alternative Price Indices 1967–2022," United States Census Bureau, Income in the United States: 2022, Report Number P60–269, September 12, 2023, https://www.census.gov/data/tables/2023/demo/income-poverty/p60-279.html;
Alex Tanzi and Bloomberg, "Inflation Was So Bad Last Year that Real Household Income Tumbled the Most in 12 Years, Causing Families Severe Economic Pain," *Fortune,* September 12, 2023, https://fortune.com/2023/09/12/real-household-income-inflation/.

debt, and the devil it can create—inflation. I hope that settles in and you can see the importance of sound fiscal policy. We have not had such a thing for a while now, and we desperately need a return to fiscal sanity.

There is another aspect of the national debt that is vital to understand. To introduce it, let me go back to the fundamentals of prosperity and what it takes to achieve it. You see, Working Man, a legitimate role and purpose of government is infrastructure. There are certain elements, bedrock items, that a society needs for peace and prosperity. You must look at foundational items, themes, to get the list right. Otherwise, government is always and forever working on the wrong things.

I find it profound and not at all accidental that our principles from Chapter 1 are still at work, even when, and especially when, we discuss the proper role of government. You must look to bedrock ideas, themes that run deep and wide, to understand what a well-governed people should expect and what good governance looks like.

At the most foundational level, what is the first and most important thing necessary for an economy to develop? What must be in place to secure any chance at creating prosperity? There is one thing that stands above all else if you care about an increasing standard of living: clear, well-defined, and secure private property rights.

Without knowing what belongs to each of us respectively, we cannot buy, sell, or trade. Commerce cannot proceed. This is the foundation of any and every successful economy.

Take a look back at Figure 3 in Chapter 6, Working Man. This is where we traced the path of economic development that countries go through, with the associated impacts and demands on the workforce. Look at the left-hand column again. Without private property rights, we will crash and burn right up that column to the tribal/nomadic phase, right back to the start of humanity. We will do nothing but fight over who owns what and who gets to use it. Tribal warfare is the destiny of any people abandoning property rights.

Now, Working Man, think this through in our modern times, in the United States, right here, right now. If we do not address present status and trend, there is a clear, logical end to the downward spiral of national debt. If we keep the same path, endless deficits and debt, the trail ends at one place: there is no such thing as private property.

If public sector financial obligations overwhelm private assets, then what do you really own, Working Man? Is it yours in any sense? I dare you to convince yourself that a public sector bureaucrat won't confiscate, tax, and otherwise control whatever they need to feed the public appetite. You are fool if you do.

Sometimes it is useful to run current trends out as if they were to continue unabated. That gives an important perspective and informs what we should do now. The weight and heft of the federal government and its current reach of financial obligations must be brought to heel. Freedom and prosperity depend on it.

As I've said, Working Man, you don't need a long list of things to mull over in the realm of politics. It's a brief, concise list, just a few key policy items, but you need to understand that list well. It affects directly your ability to pursue dreams, achieve them, and create the legacy that fills your life with meaning.

In the end it is immoral for any government to act as though income and property belong first to itself. The public sector does not create wealth. The private sector does. Government extracts wealth from private entities to fund its endeavors, and at substantial cost.

The cost of pitching a dollar into the federal coffer is well beyond negligible. Bureaucrats like to be paid just for hanging around. You will easily find studies showing the cost of government overhead in the 37% to 77% range. An overhead cost ratio (calculated as overhead costs ÷ total cost) of 40%–50% is very common.

An overhead ratio of 50.7% is directed by a memo from the Office of Management and Budget as recently as fiscal year 2019, set by revised policy on July 8, 1993. It's still in use. Why not? That's a sweet surcharge. Examples used in this writing are overhead for government sponsored academic research and Department of Defense contracting.[83]

Let's use 50% for convenience. So you—being a good, law-abiding, patriotic citizen—drop your hard-earned cash in the federal collection plate as it passes by. The politician running for office told you repeatedly of all the good and noble things you are funding. The nation can't get by without your cash, a burden every honest citizen must bear, so we are told.

What that beloved politician didn't tell you was that nary more than half of your collection plate offering will make it to the initiatives the pol droned on about. Half will go to the good friends the pol hired to work in the administrative state, overseeing all the government that your funds have purchased. The government must be managed, don't you know, and who better to manage it than friends, acquaintances, and connected parties to the person elected to office?

<hr>

[83] Colleen Cordes, "Colleges Struggle to Answer Tough Questions About Rates for the Overhead Costs of Government Research," *Chronicle of Higher Education* 37, no. 32 (April 24, 1991): A21, https://www.chronicle.com/article/colleges-struggle-to-answe r-questions-about-rates-for-the-overhead-costs-of-government-sponsored-research/; "Overhead Rate Methodology," Office of Management and Budget, Circular A-25, revised July 8, 1993, https://www2.fmc.gov/readingroom/docs/20-18/20-18_FY20_Overhead_Rate_Methodology.pdf/; Paulo M. Falcao, "Overhead Allocation and Marginal Cost in U.S. and Brazilian Defense Contracting," Calhoun: Institutional Archive of Naval Postgraduate School, Dudley Knox Library, December 1993, https://hdl.handle.net/10945/27197.

Are you mad yet, Working Man? I stay that way, perpetually. Welcome to the club. And it gets worse, or better, depending on which side of the tax collection plate you stand. After your coercively donated funds are whittled down by half, we get to the actual program that you funded. And we run straight into waste and fraud.[84]

Philip Bump of *The Washington Post* quotes Gallup polls showing Americans believe the government wastes 51 cents on every dollar of federal funds. Bump then proceeds to berate American citizens for having such a backward and ill-informed view.[85] This is precisely the attitude you would expect from a *Washington Post* talking head.

Bump quotes measured waste and fraud rates of 1.7%, 13%, 4.07%, 3%, 8.5%, etc., from various program audits, intending to undermine the 51% finding. Setting aside any questions regarding the veracity of government audits, the fox watching the henhouse, as the old saying goes, what Bump doesn't mention is that survey respondents are very likely including overhead costs of programs in their survey responses, costs which occur prior to any observed waste and fraud measured by an audit. If overlap between overhead and fraud is 100%, which is not likely, then survey respondents have their estimate dead-on. With any overlap number less than 100%, American opinion is optimistic. There is good reason to accept the Gallup survey results.[86]

That's right, Working Man. You are looking at a serious setback in expectations every time you send that check to the feds. And we aren't done yet. We haven't talked about corruption. Ah, yes, the

---

[84] Juhohn Lee, "The Federal Government Wastes at Least $247 Billion in Taxpayer Money Each Year. Here's How," CNBC Personal Finance, last updated May 24, 2023, https://www.cnbc.com/2023/04/18/heres-how-the-federal-government-wastes-tax-money.html;
Philip Bump, "Americans Think 51 Percent of Every Tax Dollar is Wasted. Come On, Guys," *Washington Post*, September 19, 2014, https://www.washingtonpost.com/news/the-fix/wp/2014/09/19/americans-think-51-percent-of-every-tax-dollar-is-wasted-come-on-guys/.

[85] Bump, "Americans Think 51 Percent of Every Tax Dollar is Wasted. Come On, Guys."

[86] Bump, "Americans Think 51 Percent of Every Tax Dollar is Wasted. Come On, Guys."

corruption. If I cover that, our book will become encyclopedic in volume. The strongest, most compelling argument against government is … government. Just look at what it does.

I usually come around to the same question in a discussion like this: "Why do we keep funding these clowns?" They only go to Washington and act the way they do, a complete clown's circus, because we pay them to do so. If we didn't fund it, they wouldn't go.

We have a national election every two years. It is completely in our hands to change the very fabric of government, especially the feds. Looking at the past several years of elective government in our great nation, we don't need all that many more votes. A mere 5% to 7% of the electorate would bring sweeping change to our federal machinery. I'm hoping to reach that 5%–7% with this writing.

Remember this, Working Man, when it comes to the federal government, there is no such thing as government stimulus, only government services. There are a few things that only government can do—legitimate, well-defined, properly justified public goods with no alternative. This is also a short list, just like the list of policy items you need to concern yourself with, and the feds should be constrained to that list and nothing more. We can say it succinctly. With government spending, it should be as little as possible, as local as possible. Just enough, and no more.

I can hear your thoughts, Working Man. "So, what is on the list? What do you think the federal government should be limited to?" Just because you asked, I will answer the question. Here's my honest view.

Remember, I'm referring strictly to the federal government. It is the farthest removed, least accountable governing body we have with respect to the citizens. Therefore, the federal government should be on the shortest leash, given the shortest list of demands with the most restrictive boundaries.

Here's my list:

- **National defense**, including border security. This one is easy. There is no alternative. If we are to have adequate defense of our nation, the federal government is the only institution capable of providing it. National defense is a true public good.

- **Department of Energy (DOE)**. This one may surprise you. DOE safeguards our nation's nuclear arsenal and related activities. This function is a must have. However, I am referring to this function only, the national defense aspect. I'm not referring to alternative-fuel vehicles, gene research and therapy, nanoscience, or transportation technologies. Yes, this is all in the DOE's current mission statement, and more.[87]

Deep review is needed to get DOE back to federal priorities, those that don't crush our nation under a debt burden. The descriptors you read above may possibly mask defense initiatives. Nanotechnology weapons? Gene-altering WMDs? I have no idea and I doubt most taxpayers do either. Scope creep is a skill and specialty of the federal apparatus. It may be that proper review and restructure requires rolling DOE, under a legitimate mission statement, into the Department of Defense.

DOE may be pursuing advanced, foundational scientific research that benefits all humanity, which is a true public good of critical importance, or it may be funding clandestine weapons programs threatening humanity's continued existence. Politicians and bureaucrats will talk always of the former and obfuscate always the latter. Examining

---

87 "About the US Department of Energy," Office of the Chief Human Capital Officer, downloaded 16 March 2024, https://www.energy.gov/hc/about-us-department-energy.

the far reaches, dark alleys, and back rooms of the federal labyrinth is a difficult task to satisfy.

Nonetheless, in an ocean of unknowables, there stands a beacon of pure, lucid, piercing light, calling us home, guiding us to right action. This beacon signals one thing we can know with certainty—we are spending ourselves into oblivion.

- **Department of the Treasury.** As stated at length earlier, we need a sound currency. In a modern world, this is basic infrastructure, in scope for the feds.

- **National Aeronautics and Space Administration (NASA).** Redefined and restructured, by way of necessity, to include all basic, fundamental scientific research that is too risky or far reaching for private investment. As stated earlier, this is a true public good of utmost importance, properly placed at the federal level. This department will have a new name, and I wouldn't venture a guess as to what that should be.

First, before NASA is resanctioned and reformed, massive cuts must occur across a score or more of federal agencies, including wholesale closure. At present, basic science is touted across everything hither and yon: National Institutes of Health, which after COVID is the National Institute of Embarrassment, Waste, and Ineptitude; United States Department of Agriculture; DOE, as stated earlier; Department of Transportation; and on it goes.

Everyone claims money for science because it is easy to sell to the public, and no one is accountable. Federal sprawl guarantees that. A single unit at the federal level dedicated to basic scientific research is adequate, more efficient, and easier to audit.

And, well, that's it. I told you, it's a short list. I know an item you will think of soon, if not already—national parks. It's one of my favorites also. I love the national park system. I also know, given our history and experience with public parks and lands, that it can be done at the state level. It is no longer 1870, when we had little infrastructure to work with and very limited historical reference. States will have to practice up on shared contracts and agreements with other states. That's a good and necessary thing. But ...

Department of Housing and Urban Development? Why? Are we so enfeebled and dependent that we can't choose our own housing? Do we need bureaucratic oversight in our living rooms and backyards?

Department of Education? Are you joking? Every single state has a board of education.

Department of Transportation? Interstate agreements, which need to come alive like never before, nullify the need for this at the federal level. Federalism had a rough patch early in our nation's history because states refused to cooperate. If we aren't grown up enough at this point to get past that, the federal beast may never be tamed.

Bureau of Alcohol, Tobacco, and Firearms. This should be a convenience store. Yes, I know, they've added "Explosives." State level, all of it, to the extent we need it at all.

Working Man, it's time for a major housecleaning at the federal level. Entire departments can be closed, and the nation would never miss them. In the business world, we call this operational review and market discipline. Your typical bureaucrat thinks they are above such things. They believe themselves to be too important. Let's dispense with the foolish thinking that has bequeathed our country a sprawling wasteland of federal largess, tucked away on the national credit card. Read on to discover how we accomplish the task.

This exercise and discussion highlight our failure in congressional appropriations. Everyone has a list. Mine is short. A leftist has a very long list, everything imaginable, most of it illegitimate for federal purview. Members of Congress, in their typical feckless, spineless conduct, throw money at all of it. This is not sustainable, a point in fact that can no longer be sidestepped.

Politicians are always and forever striving to convince us that we need them. I have a proposition. Let's embark on a mission to discover how much government, especially at the federal level, that we can do without. I believe much can be done regarding the removal of federal expenditure, and the working American public will never miss it. Let's find out.

PROPOSALS FOR REFORM

The Tyranny of the Majority and the Great Civil Rights Struggle

What do we change, Working Man? As we look at the threat of national deficit and debt, history can inform us of both root cause and remedy. We have faced a similar problem before but in a very different context.

This exercise in government that we enjoy was officially started in 1776 by the Declaration of Independence. And it is nothing less than the most amazing political accomplishment in the history of mankind. Our government is unique and exceptional in that it was founded on a sole and singular idea: liberty. The advancement of humanity within this frame of government has been staggering in breadth, scope, reach, and depth. What an immense and amazing success.

And there have been flaws, sometimes deep and tragic. The most glaring is in the realm of civil rights—slavery. An entire race of people was kept in bondage until 1865. America's constitutional government, incredible in structure and impact, required reform to bring slavery to an end.

Fortunately, America's founding provided the framework within which these tragedies could be addressed. Unfortunately, it also required the Civil War, the Civil Rights Act of 1964, multiple constitutional amendments, and numerous social movements to remedy this historical wrong.

Slavery continued to exist enabled by what historically has been a problem bedeviling societies since the beginning of time—the Tyranny of the Majority.[88] Democratic rule, rule by majority vote, is no guarantor of peace, prosperity, or any enjoyment of civil liberties whatsoever, including life itself. The 51% majority can vote to remove any of these from the 49%, and throughout history it has often done so.[89]

A majority of voters from America's founding through to the late 1800s decided that slavery should remain. To a slave, this was a horrific crime. To a slaveowner, it was just a matter of property.

What kind of political dynamic could possibly let this exist? The Tyranny of the Majority can result in perversions of many kinds, with no justice in sight. Slavery is a miserable and disastrous example.

Thankfully, through the hard work, sacrifice, and passion of many people, slavery came to an end, and civil liberties are more exalted

---

[88] "Tyranny of the Majority," Oxford Reference, accessed March 3, 2024, https://www.oxfordreference.com/display/10.1093/oi/authority.20110803110431595.

[89] David Spitz, "On the Abuses of Power in Democratic States," *Midwest Journal of Political Science* 1, no. 3/4 (Nov. 1957): 225–232, https://doi.org/10.2307/2109301; Arlene W. Saxonhouse, "A Story of Use and Abuse: Athenian Democracy in the Political Imagination," *Lapham's Quarterly*, accessed March 3, 2024, https://www.laphamsquarterly.org/democracy/story-use-and-abuse; Mark Cartwright, s.v. "Ostracism," *World History Encyclopedia*, March 30, 2016, https://www.worldhistory.org/Ostracism/; Isidor Feinstein Stone, *The Trial of Socrates* (London: Little, Brown, 1988).

than ever before in our nation. May civil rights continue to flourish and expand. Mankind is better for it.

In an entirely different context, we have a separate problem threatening our future, with the same political dynamic at play. The Tyranny of the Majority is at it once again, taking from the minority what should be its own as guaranty.

As we stand today, politicians face no consequence whatsoever for deficit spending and debt accumulation. In fact, they are incented to do so. Their best plan for reelection is to buy votes with other people's money.

As it turns out, they are quite good at it. Promise the moon, highlight the benefits, and swing the vote, all paid for by people out of their district, at least most of it. Selling the benefits and hiding the costs are staple skills for a retail politician. A businessman wouldn't last with this strategy, but it works, apparently with no limits whatsoever, in the public realm.

With these political incentives in play, we have endless federal deficits and debt accumulation before us. Working Man, allow me to make a proposal. If we are to find an answer, find a better path, it will require a crusade similar to the civil rights movement that so enormously benefited our country.

You see, Working Man, the key to ending slavery and establishing civil liberties for all was in focusing on the individual. Harriet Tubman said it best.

> Slavery is the next thing to hell.[90]

> There are two things I've got a right to, and these
> are, Death or Liberty—one or the other I mean
> to have. No one will take me back alive; I shall

---

90   Harriet Tubman, quoted in Benjamin Drew, *A North-Side View of Slavery* (Boston: John P. Jewett and Company, 1856), 30.

> fight for my liberty, and when the time has come
> for me to go, the Lord will let them, kill me.[91]

The second quote is the most widely quoted version of the Harriet Tubman statement, but it is reworded from the original text. I love the original text so much, I'm going to include it here separately, with mid-1800s southern U.S. grammar gloriously intact.

> Dere's *two* things I've got a *right* to, and dese are,
> Death or Liberty—one or tother I mean to have.
> No one will take me back alive; I shall fight for
> my liberty, and when de time has come for me to
> go, de Lord will let dem kill me.[92]

Injustice incurred against the individual could only be corrected the same way, with freedom for the individual. Harriet Tubman's statements of truth carried the public sentiment of the day, and justice won out over the slavery argument.

A similar focus, on the individual, is now required for property rights. The Tyranny of the Majority, one federal program and one federal benefit at a time, with no end in sight, erodes our ability to earn, hold, and enjoy private property, the fruit of our labor.

Can we find answers? I believe we can. Working Man, back to our principles of problem-solving. Break it down, frame it, and solve the components one at a time.

The Tyranny of the Majority and the Protection of Prosperity

Let's jump in, Working Man. How might we frame and address the Tyranny of the Majority with respect to property rights?

---

91   Harriet Tubman, quoted in Sarah H. Bradford, *Scenes in the Life of Harriet Tubman* (Auburn, NY: W. J. Moses, 1869), 21.

92   Harriet Tubman, quoted in Sarah H. Bradford, *Scenes in the Life of Harriet Tubman*, 21.

It is possible to build policies that actually work, those that preserve freedom, prosperity, and the ability to enjoy the work of our own hands. I believe America's best days are ahead of it, so let's put our hands to the plow and get it done.

To start with, let's understand the political conflict we see today. Here is a statement that should crystallize the situation in your mind with resolute clarity: There is no more rapacious and unprincipled capitalist than a socialist. Oh, yes, you heard me right, Working Man. A socialist, or leftist, pick your term, is actually a straight-up capitalist.

Leftists are profit motivated just like anyone else; they just want to use federal authority to implement their business plans. You and I have to build customer loyalty through quality products, competitive pricing, and excellent service to achieve our goals. The leftists find that slow and annoying. They believe it is beneath them. They prefer to use the appropriate federal agency to command their just and proper control of profit flows in what would otherwise be an open economy, with open competition.

It's common to hear talk these days of a second American civil war.[93] Personally, I think the chances of such a thing are right at zero. We may dislike each other over political and cultural views, it seems clear that we do, but we have never loved our individual civil liberties more. And I don't see anyone willing to give those up

---

[93] Barbara F. Walter, *How Civil Wars Start: and How to Stop Them* First Edition (New York: Crown, 2022);
"BU Historian Answers: Are We Headed for Another Civil War?," *BU Today*, Boston University, March 27, 2019, https://www.bu.edu/articles/2019/are-we-headed-for-another-civil-war/;
William Howell and Paul Rand, "Is the U.S. Headed Toward Another Civil War?," January 5, 2023, in *Big Brains*, produced by the University of Chicago, podcast, MP3 audio, 30:35, https://news.uchicago.edu/us-headed-toward-another-civil-war-william-howell;
Bruce Stokes, "Could the United States be Headed for a National Divorce?," Chatham House, February 20, 2024, https://www.chathamhouse.org/2024/02/could-united-states-be-headed-national-divorce.

or fighting to take them from someone else—not on the scale of a national civil war. This demonstrated, shared, and deepening love for civil liberties is a recipe for beautiful, stable liberty. Live and let live. God Bless the United States. May she live forever.

However, I think the chances of suffering a catastrophic national crisis—most likely financial in nature, because we lack the political cohesion that musters the national will to foresee and implement preventive measures—are near 100%. Such a catastrophe could also come in the form of a foreign war that we can't fight and win properly because our national debt ties our hands. A calamity along these lines is not only possible but it is also fast becoming a certainty.

However, you know what, Working Man? It hasn't happened yet, so let's get to work on solving the problem before us. That's what we are made for. God put us here exactly for that reason.

I'm going to list out below policy proposals that are serious and address the problem before us. I will also address political realities inside each one, not to undermine the viability of an idea but to prepare the ground for changes in thinking that are necessary to get the reform in place that we need. We've all heard it said: "That will never pass. Nobody will vote for that." Maybe so, but it's time to get past that easy dismissal. We have a crisis in front of us.

1. The very first item, and this one, Working Man, is of the utmost importance:

    o   Balanced-budget amendment to the U.S. Constitution

I'm not sure any idea deserves more urgent attention and political action than this one. Congress can no longer be trusted standalone with the nation's finances for a simple reason: Congress is the problem. As stated earlier, the incentives are hopelessly bent against responsibility. Restraint must be brought to bear with force of law.

And I'm referring to an amendment with teeth. I would propose the following language:

> The United States Congress shall not allow total outlays in a fiscal year to exceed total revenues for that same fiscal year. Any member of Congress not voting in accordance with this balanced-budget amendment shall be subject to an immediate felony charge of criminal theft with a prison term of no less than five years. There shall be a single exception to this balanced-budget amendment: during times of armed conflict when, and only when, the United States Congress has passed a formal declaration of war, according to constitutional procedure and requirements.

And that would do it, Working Man. Suddenly, members of Congress are responsible. It's amazing what incentives can do.

2. Here's a second idea, worthy of serious thought and consideration:

   o   Constitutional amendment limiting federal spending to a fixed percentage of GDP

This idea carries heft, Working Man. Some say 18% is the right number. We currently stand at 23% for the latest report in 2023.[94] Let's get into the next idea, and we will discuss this further.

3. Consider another serious idea:

   o   Constitutional amendment limiting the national debt to GDP ratio

---

[94]   "How Much Has the U.S. Government Spent This Year?," FiscalData, U.S. Department of the Treasury, last updated September 30, 2023, https://fiscaldata. treasury.gov/americas-finance-guide/federal-spending/.

This idea, and the second idea above, are different methods of the same proposal—limit overall spending and debt in relation to the size and growth of the U.S. economy. The merit of these ideas is compelling—impose authoritative and forceful limits on spending while also recognizing that economic growth gives flexibility with regard to government services.

My personal view would be to pass the first item with urgency, right away, and then wait for the need and purpose to clarify the second and third items. However, if political cohesion coalesces around all three together, or any combination including the first item, so be it.

4. This idea undoes what I believe to be a mistake in history:

    o   Repeal of the 16th Amendment to the U.S. Constitution

The 16th Amendment cast aside state apportionment of funds to the federal government and allowed for a direct federal tax upon income. In my personal view, this is a joint economic and political disaster for two reasons.

First of all, the taxing of income is a gross distortion of incentives. Personal income is personal property and should not be subject to taxation. Your financial gains in life are yours first, not the feds' first, with you retaining the leftovers. We've reached the point where personal income is seldom viewed as what it actually is— personal property. That is a tragedy. Personal income is how you take care of yourself and your loved ones. The government should have no right to direct taxation upon the source of your material well-being.

There's a general view that income is apportioned first to the federal government, then wage earners subsequently own only the portion remaining. I do not believe it is coincidental that this view grows alongside the view that government is a constant, necessary, and ever-increasing source of financial sustenance and benefit. I believe these views ascend together for a reason. Both views are descendants of the 16th Amendment—together they are a cancer threatening our culture and social fabric. The federal government has become our parent.

These views are not sustainable. The proper view, which should be held sacred, is that your income is your personal property, from which your physical and financial needs are met. The 16th Amendment must be repealed.

Secondly, the federal government is no longer bound to states for revenue. State apportionment requires that funds for federal initiatives pass first through the states and then to federal coffers. Localizing government, especially taxation, is a big part of any solution to our current national indebtedness. This would be a good place to start—reestablish state apportionment.

5. With this idea, we drive a stake through the heart of the Tyranny of the Majority:

    o   Require a supermajority vote—I suggest two-thirds— of Senate and House members to increase federal levies or raise the debt limit.

Finally, with this idea, we fully acknowledge the ridiculous and overwhelming incentive a member of Congress has to waste our money on everything in sight. In the face of political division, Congress has resorted to throwing money in all directions. No priorities, no budgeting, no debates—just toss cash with whimsy and survive the next election. We can't live that way, Working Man. That is no way to govern a serious nation, and we will cease to be a serious nation if we keep this up.

6. If you question the profound insight of the Founding Fathers of the United States, just look at this one:

    o   U.S. Constitution Article V states convention

It's as though the writers, signers, and architects of the U.S. Constitution were looking forward in time and wrote this article just for us. They could see a time and circumstance when perverse incentives would freeze members of Congress and prevent sensible and necessary legislation. We are now at that point. Congress has created a problem that it cannot fix, that it has no desire or will to fix. Article V allows for direct address of such a circumstance. States can call for a constitutional convention allowing for the proposal of amendments, and Congress has no choice but to comply.

Article V is so short and powerful, I will quote it here for ease of reference:

> The Congress, whenever two thirds of both houses shall deem it necessary, shall propose Amendments to this Constitution, or, on the application of the Legislatures of two-thirds of the several States, shall call a Convention for proposing Amendments, which, in either Case, shall be valid to all Intents and Purposes, as Part of this Constitution, when ratified by the Legislatures of three fourths of the several States, or by Conventions in three fourths thereof, as the one or the other Mode of Ratification may be proposed by the Congress; provided that no Amendment which may be made prior to the Year One thousand eight hundred and eight shall in any Manner affect the first and fourth Clauses in the Ninth Section of the first Article; and that no State, without its Consent, shall be deprived of its equal Suffrage in the Senate.
>
> United States Constitution, Article V

I think, beyond doubt, that it is better for any or all of the first five ideas to come through the normal channel for constitutional amendments: Congressional vote. However, I also think a states convention is a legitimate, and possibly crucial, leverage point. It may be required to force the issue. My belief is that if an Article V states convention is imminent, Congress will act and do its job. I think that would be a great outcome and use of this option.

Let's put on the full-court press, Working Man. If this is what it takes to galvanize Congress, so be it.

7. These next two ideas are right at the top of the nobody-will-vote-for-this list. And I don't care. It's time to address foundational weaknesses.

    o   "You vote for it, you pay for it."

I'm well aware of a politician's dodgy, spineless behavior. They are nothing more than optimizing agents seeking votes. I'm well aware of the ease with which ideas are demonized and discarded in this competition for votes.

I'm also aware of a fatal flaw in our body politic, a flaw that is about to destroy us. In present form, the majority of politicians in legislatures and the majority of individual voters in the polling booth, when casting votes, are thinking primarily of benefits and not of costs. How else do you get a national debt of current enormity?

We must consider alternative habits and methods that force consideration, at the point of casting a vote, of full costs and full benefits of any public proposal. I give you an idea for consideration.

With current database technology, it is easy to freeze jurisdictional geographic boundaries in place at the time a House vote is held. If a U.S. House member votes to pass a fiscal initiative, the district hosting that House member should be allocated both the benefits and costs of that initiative. The district of each and every House member voting against that same initiative will receive neither the costs nor the benefits.

This method will accomplish the goal of forcing consideration of both costs and benefits at the proper point in time—when the votes are cast. This idea carries a second benefit, a benefit of enormous scope and import: the sorting out of true public goods versus ideas merely sold as public goods.

You see, Working Man, the idea of a "public good" is inherently an economic concept that has been hijacked by politics. A true public good is an essential product or service that, once produced, is not divisible into distinct units; therefore, it cannot be priced and sold in a common-air market. The classic, and indisputably true, example is national defense. Once the United States is properly defended, you cannot separate units of national defense and sell to the buying public.

We are either all defended or none of us are. There is no "carton" of national defense waiting on the shelf at Costco. The proper and efficient method is to tax each citizen of the U.S. and provide for a common national defense.

Politicians, of course, have observed the immense opportunity here, and now declare everything under the sun to be a public good. They beguile the voter with full knowledge of the deception. They know what they are doing.

A prime example of a fake public good is health care, or health care insurance. Either aspect, direct health care or insurance to support health care, is easily divisible into individual units and sold in standard market form. Two things government at any level, local, state, or federal, should never be entrusted with are product design and product pricing. A bureaucrat has no means or incentive to accomplish either one in a competent or honest fashion. Proper discernment, then, between true public goods and fraudulent offerings thereof will help keep government actors focused strictly on true public good, their only legitimate domain.

With a "you vote for it, you pay for it" methodology, the tax structure of every House district will be in play at every election. Don't think that won't matter, Working Man. It will have a great impact—and all toward the benefit of returning us to fiscal soundness and sanity.

8.   Here's the next audacious, brash nobody-will-vote-for-this idea:

    o   A flat fee for federal taxes

A flat tax rate is often floated as an avant-garde tax-reform idea. It isn't nearly avant-garde enough. We need something more bold and more effective.

Working Man, the problem addressed in idea 7 above is actually worse than described there. Not only do voters stand in a voting booth, or members of Congress in session, and cast votes thinking of benefits and not costs, but many voters, a bunch, also pay no federal tax at all (Appendix, Figure 19).[95] They have zero total federal tax burden.

---

[95]   David Splinter, "Who Pays No Tax? The Declining Fraction Paying Income Taxes and Increasing Tax Progressivity," *Contemporary Economic Policy* 37, no. 3 (July 2019): 413–26, https://doi.org/10.1111/coep.12407;
Roberton Williams, "Who Pays No Income Tax: A 2013 Update," *Tax Notes,* The Tax Policy Center, Urban Institute and Brookings Institution, September 30, 2013, https://www.urban.org/sites/default/files/publication/23171/1001697-Who-Pays-No-Income-Tax-A-Update.PDF;
Roberton Williams, "Who Pays No Income Tax," *Tax Notes,* The Tax Policy Center, Urban Institute and Brookings Institution, June 29, 2009: 1583, https://www.tax-notes.com/tax-notes-federal/credits/who-pays-no-income-tax/2009/06/29/qg0w;
Scott Hodge, "40 Million Filers Pay No Income Taxes, Many Get Generous Refunds," Tax Foundation, June 5, 2003, https://taxfoundation.org/data/all/federal/40-million-filers-pay-no-income-taxes-many-get-generous-refunds/;
Don Fullerton and Nirupama S. Rao, "The Lifecycle of the 47%," (working paper no. 22580, National Bureau of Economic Research, Cambridge, MA, August 2016), http://www.nber.org/papers/w22580.

Back to basics. Is the federal government the domain of public goods or not? If so, and public goods are provided, then the public should pay—all of us.

Assessing federal programs and benefits shouldn't differ much from a trip to a local retail store. I get a receipt, a list of purchased items, with a cost next to it. If I'm happy, I come back. If I'm not happy, I change my shopping habits.

Each voter, and member of Congress, should be aware of the programs they are receiving or supporting, and the cost of each, along with the total tax burden. The combination of ideas 7 and 8 guarantee that individual program costs and the associated total tax burden will be accounted for at each and every vote.

With many voters having no federal tax burden and considering primarily program benefits rather than costs, what outcome would you expect, Working Man? Maybe a burgeoning national debt with no end in sight? Yep, that's what you would expect, and that is what we have. Incentives, once again, reign supreme.

Pay a per-head fee for national initiatives with a line-item receipt in front of you. That will change our course—absolutely for the better.

If any voter, including me, wants a lower tax burden, we should, each of us, vote for fewer or more-efficient programs. We should not, under any circumstance, vote to move that burden to someone else. And by God's almighty hand of justice, we should never hire a politician to shift that burden for us. God help us.

Critics will lampoon the idea as regressive taxation. Call it that if you like. It is also fair and effective. Every voting member of this great republic should consider the overall tax burden and specific program costs and benefits when casting a vote. If the burden is always borne by someone else, how can that ever happen? Might we suffer the Tyranny of the Majority? What could go wrong?

9. Now we go populist, Working Man. Power to the people.

    o   A line-item veto on the congressional federal budget
        voted on every two years with each national election

Why not? We've been stealing from fellow citizens for decades now, including from generations of citizens not yet born. How much fiscal profligacy do you wish to burden your great-grandchildren with?

Technology makes a voting process of this nature easy. Electronic ballots are commonplace. Plowing through a full federal budget on Election Day is not a small task, but it's time to man up and face what we've done.

Our federal government is out of control. Let's place each item before the public and vote. Congressional expenditures are approved now on strictly a simple majority-vote basis, and Tyranny of the Majority is already in play. Critics will say this idea reverses said tyranny to now be against federal programs. I say to that, "It's about time."

I'm well aware of the argument that having reasoned debate among elected representatives will bring more expertise and sensible decision-making to budget choices, as opposed to raw, popular vote. That's a great argument, until you take even the most casual look at how Congress wastes our money.

I'm not convinced that reasoning, debate, expertise, or sensibility—or any adult characteristic of any variety for that matter—has any relation to congressional appropriations. Congress has lost credibility. Take it to the ballot box.

10. Here's a perennial favorite of the conservative crowd, Working Man:

    o   Congressional term limits for U.S. House and U.S.
        Senate seats

I will offer my personal view on this one. I am not opposed, per se, and if it comes up for a vote, I will support it. However, honestly, I do not think this idea will be very effective.

I see it this way. A member of Congress can do an awful lot of damage in two years. Term limits alone will not change the basic incentives and dynamics we see in play today. Without reforms discussed in ideas 1 through 9 above, I don't think term limits will change much of anything.

One large caveat, though, is that if the body politic, common voters, are heartened and encouraged by the fact that patronage, corruption, and ne'er-do-well congressional reps face a limit on how deep they can embed themselves in the public apparatus, then I'm all for it. There is something to be said for voters giving a firm thumbs-down to long-term, public-office benefaction. If the voting public wants to make Cincinnatus[96] the official model, count me in.

Working Man, this is the revolution in front of us now—the protection of prosperity through a civil rights movement focused on property rights. Can I enjoy what I have built? Is it mine, or does someone else have first claim?

Your legacy, Working Man, that thing you build over a lifetime to bequeath, is empty without secure property rights. In its current state, as of today, the voting public, through vacuous and endless borrowing and debt, has been allowed to trample the rights of the individual. The Tyranny of the Majority is in effect. That must stop. Right now.

---

[96] *Funk and Wagnalls New World Encyclopedia*, World Book, Inc., (2018), s.v. "Cincinnatus, Lucius Quinctius";
Encyclopedia *Britannica*, s.v. "Lucius Quinctius Cincinnatus," last modified January 31, 2024, https://www.britannica.com/biography/Lucius-Quinctius-Cincinnatus;
Donald L. Wasson, s.v. "Cincinnatus," *World History Encyclopedia*, April 4, 2017, https://www.worldhistory.org/Cincinnatus/.

The travesties associated with the Tyranny of the Majority have been referred to, perhaps tongue in cheek, as "other devils."[97] Other devils, indeed. To all human beings, past and present, who have been deprived of personal rights and property because it was politically feasible, socially acceptable, or because someone just felt good about it, convinced the deprived party deserved it, the term "other devils" is packed with meaning. There is no tyranny greater or crueler than that driven by a sense of righteousness. God help us to wake up and realize what we are doing to ourselves and our neighbors.

Secure individual property rights are the civil rights issue of our day. As generations past have done in this great republic, the United States of America, may we comprehend the challenge and step up to it. I pray we are up to the task.

---

[97] J.R. Hicks, *The Social Framework: An Introduction to Economics*, 2nd ed. (Oxford: The Clarendon Press, 1952), 218.

Chapter 8

LIES EXPOSED AND TRUTH DISCOVERED

WORKING MAN, SHUN lies and embrace the truth—a good maxim to live by. To use an old farm quote, we've cut a wide swath here. We've waded through normal, everyday modern life in our book excursion, and along the way, we've exposed a number of lies and pointed the way to truth. Here's a summary of major points, modern lies commonly held, and the truth to live by:

Big Lie #1: Problems in life are a hassle. Avoid them.

The Truth: Problems are a gift, Working Man. Solve them and reap the rewards.

Big Lie #2: God looks on coldly, cool and detached, while the world suffers; therefore, He stands condemned. If He even exists at all, I cannot trust Him.

The Truth: His name is Emmanuel, God With Us. He feels everything we feel. He suffers right along with us. He is right there next to us in all stations of life: good, bad, high, low, just, unjust, pleasant, or miserable. God has a plan as to when this present unjust world should end. Leave that to Him. In the meantime, He asks us to live by faith. God cares about you, Working Man, and He proves it by walking with you every second of every day, fully sharing in all of life's troubles and triumphs.

Big Lie #3: I am the captain of my soul.

The Truth: Okay, captain, that's big talk for someone who can't guarantee their next breath. Yea, so much for controlling your destiny. You don't even know if you will make the dinner table tonight. The truth is that I am put on this earth as a steward, and I control only one thing: my choice in the moment, what I say and do right now. And that is plenty; it's all I need. I accept my status in life and get on with doing my best, doing all the good that I can possibly do. It is an amazing, productive life.

Big Lie #4: Modern marriages just can't last. People go their own way.

The Truth: Marriage is designed by the Almighty to be lifelong, and the benefits are immense, reaching generation to generation. Financially, emotionally, socially, physically, in every way, humankind is best served by lifelong marriages.

Big Lie #5: Sex and love are separate areas of life and should be managed accordingly.

The Truth: Sex and love are designed by God as an intricately woven strand, a finely braided rope. The benefit of understanding and living this way is a treasure beyond description: intimacy. It is pleasure, tenderness, joy, affection, satisfaction, solace, contentment, and comfort like nothing you have known, and something you cannot obtain any other way. It is just plain fun with lifelong delight thrown in. It is Divine, God's plan from the beginning. It is Heaven on Earth.

Big Lie #6: Marriage grows stale over time. This is the normal burden and cost of a lifelong relationship.

The Truth: Marriage is alive and vibrant. The pleasure to be enjoyed has no end and no boundary, no constraint on height or depth. Ascension or descension in a marriage is a choice, Working Man. Ascension is the original plan by design and will be yours to have if you live by principle. You will not be the same, granted, your character will change from the core, through and through, but all for the better. Descension happens due to the improper choices of the participant.

Big Lie #7: The raising of children is complex to the point of being impossible to understand. Only educated experts can get a handle on it.

The Truth: There is method to the madness—foundational principles can be understood and properly applied. The average Working Man and Working Woman can both comprehend the principles involved and get the job done. It is hard work, to be sure, but clarity of mind can be achieved, and that 18 years or so of investment in the next generation can pay off extraordinarily.

Big Lie #8: Honesty and hard work do not pay off in today's economy. You need connections, and you should do whatever it takes to get them. Character is old fashioned, out of date, and in the way.

The Truth: Lack of integrity guarantees failure for you and everyone working around you. Foundational principles can be understood in the workplace and used for great success.

Big Lie #9: Keynesian economic theory proves that government spending provides fiscal stimulus benefiting all Americans.

The Truth: Keynesian economic theory is a hoax, disproving itself. Keynes himself knew this and brushed it aside. Keynesian theory and endless deficit spending is a religion that will end as all bad religions do—when adequate exposure forces adherents to abandon the faith. The consequent damage may be staggering, but the outcome is determined. Truth will win out. May we wise up as soon as possible.

Big Lie #10: Change is threatening, unwelcome, and almost always negative. Change should be avoided and resisted.

The Truth: Change is an unavoidable fact of life. I cannot choose to avoid change. It will happen whether I like it or not. But I can choose the direction. With a proper approach, change can have me on an upward spiral, steadily improving. With an improper approach, I will spiral downward, steadily deteriorating.

Big Lie #11: Morality is an old fashioned, outdated idea. It's just someone else trying to run your life with their rules. Pay no heed.

The Truth: Many problems in life are moral in nature. The need for a moral framework is intrinsic, manifest, and unavoidable. Choose the framework carefully, with deep thought and sincere consideration. Morality does not work if it is "someone else's rules." It is only effective when it is internal to the deciding agent. When internalized, a moral frame is of great worth.

CLOSE

Working Man, we've had quite a journey together. We have covered some very big ideas, a lot of territory. As I said, we have cut a wide swath. Thank you for joining me. I hope you have enjoyed the conversation as much as I have. Most of all, I hope the Working Woman in your life finds benefit. I hope you treat her better due to all that we have discussed.

As we close this book, take this thought with you and may it never leave you: Make peace with your Creator and live in His service. This is why you were made, and it is the purpose of Eternity. God's blessings be upon you.

Acknowledgments

MY DEAREST WIFE, Melissa, what can I possibly say? I can't be me without you, Babe. Thank you for the most precious gift that you could have ever given me—you.

Thank you to my parents, Don and Dona Teague. You gave me the most important thing in life—character.

Thank you to my children. The gifts you have given are numerous but let's be honest and focus on the truly important one—grandchildren.

Thank you to Bovina Independent School District, West Texas State University, and Oklahoma State University. You gave me a great education and something that has proven to be of high worth—skills.

Thank you to the hundreds of colleagues I had the good fortune to work with over the years. The experiences and friendships we shared were, and continue to be, a treasure.

Thank you to the Book Launchers team. You opened my eyes to so many valuable tools and techniques. Your support has been fantastic and deeply appreciated.

Thank you to my brothers. Life would be a complete bore without you.

Thank you to our American forbears for this great nation and all it stands for. Thank you for every hardship that you bore, every insight that you bequeathed, every improvement that you left behind and, most of all, thank you for the vision to become the envy of the modern world. May we be worthy of your heritage.

Thank you to the Almighty for Your wondrous creation and the grace to enjoy it each day.

Appendix

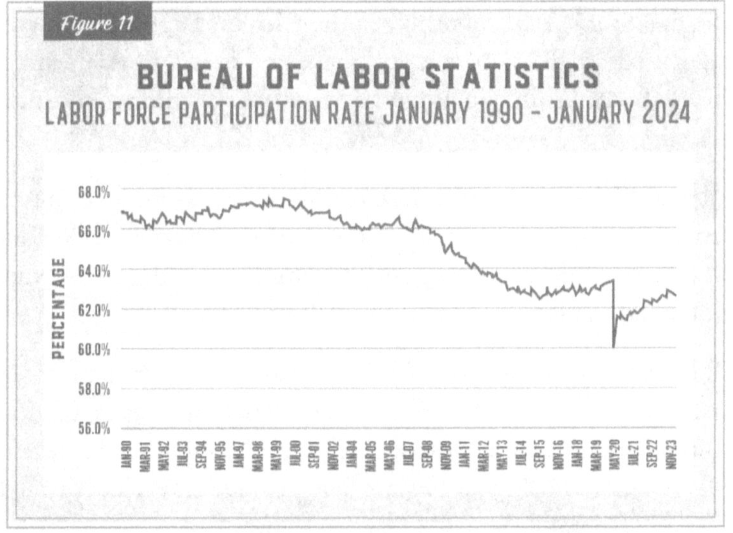

DATA FROM "CIVILIAN LABOR FORCE PARTICIPATION RATE," U.S. BUREAU OF LABOR STATISTICS, ACCESSED APRIL 24, 2024, HTTPS://WWW.BLS.GOV/CHARTS/ EMPLOYMENT-SITUATION/CIVILIAN-LABOR-FORCE-PARTICIPATION-RATE.HTM.

THE CHART ABOVE displays public data published by the Bureau of Labor Statistics (BLS), Department of Labor. The chart uses the standard BLS definition of "civilian labor force participation rate," which is data series LNS12000000, the seasonally adjusted number of individuals employed age 16 or older, added to data series LNS13000000, the seasonally adjusted number of individuals unemployed but actively looking for work, age 16 or older. This sum is divided by the total civilian noninstitutional population, age 16 and older, data series LNU00000000. Noninstitutional excludes active-duty military and people confined to or living in facilities such as jails, prisons, detention centers, or residential care centers.

Mathematically, the formula is this: labor force participation rate = ((data series LNS12000000 + data series LNS13000000) + data series LNU00000000).

The data is gathered monthly via the Current Population Survey conducted by BLS. Essentially, the chart shows the percentage of able-bodied individuals age 16 or over, excluding active-duty military, who are working or actively looking for work.

A lot of hard work went into creating the peak number you see above of about 67%. That is down now to about 62%. That 5-point gap represents roughly 13.5 million people, able-bodied individuals no longer even trying to find work.

One could easily argue that 67% is too low; 72% is not an unreasonable target, even 80%. If you accept those possibilities, the 13.5 million count becomes two or three times as high. And I have to ask the question: "How many are being paid to stay home through state and federal benefits?" I fear the answer.

We are losing our work culture. Changes need to happen and soon.

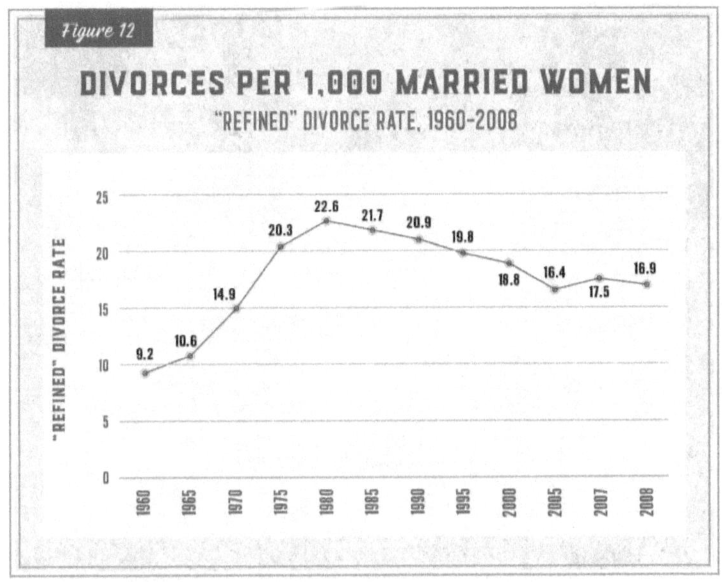

DATA FROM W. BRADFORD WILCOX, *STATE OF OUR UNIONS*, NATIONAL MARRIAGE PROJECT, DECEMBER 2009, 75.

The term "refined" refers to the method of sampling. A refined divorce rate takes the number of divorces in a year, divided by the number of married women age 15 and over in that year. This "refines" the divorce rate by focusing on the population that is susceptible to divorce, versus the entire population, where many are not married. This number reflects the annual divorce rate, not a lifetime divorce rate. The references listed in Chapters 1 and 4 discuss the many complexities with this number.

Figure 13

U.S. SERVICES AND GOODS-PRODUCING INDUSTRIES, 2017–2022

DESCRIPTION	2017	2018	2019	2020	2021	2022
Total GDP—All Industries-1	34,468.1	35,461.5	36,120.5	34,938.6	37,216.6	38,062.5
Private Goods-Producing Industries-2	8,166.3	8,372.9	8,350.3	7,921.3	8,138.2	8,086.9
Total Services, Including Gov't.	26,301.8	27,088.6	27,770.2	27,017.3	29,078.4	29,975.6
Private Goods Produced, % of Total:	23.7%	23.6%	23.1%	22.7%	21.9%	21.2%
Service Sector, Incl Gov't, % of Total:	76.3%	76.4%	76.9%	77.3%	78.1%	78.8%

1. CHAINED (2017) DOLLAR SERIES ARE CALCULATED AS THE PRODUCT OF THE CHAIN-TYPE QUANTITY INDEX AND THE 2017 CURRENT-DOLLAR VALUE OF THE CORRESPONDING SERIES, DIVIDED BY 100.

2. CONSISTS OF AGRICULTURE, FORESTRY, FISHING, AND HUNTING; MINING; CONSTRUCTION; AND MANUFACTURING.

DATA FROM "REAL GROSS OUTPUT BY INDUSTRY, BILLIONS OF 2017 CHAINED DOLLARS," U.S. BUREAU OF ECONOMIC ANALYSIS, SEPTEMBER 28, 2023, HTTPS://WWW.BEA.GOV/DATA/INDUSTRIES/GROSS-OUTPUT-BY-INDUSTRY.

The table above is taken straight from Bureau of Economic Analysis data, modified only to focus on the totals, service, and nonservice sectors. The footnotes are as written by the bureau, shortened to what is relevant for the data listed. The service sector above is essentially defined as everything other than private goods-producing industries, including a small undefined category.

As you can see, Working Man, the service sector is strong and showing no signs of abatement. The sector dominates our economy. This is proof positive of a highly developed economy full of diverse opportunity, driven by consumers and producers free to choose. I would offer one caution. Avoid the most annoying, and potentially damaging, of modern habits—don't forget upon whose shoulders we stand. Without those goods-producing sectors (agriculture, fishing, mining, etc.) and disposable income, there would be no service sector.

CATEGORIES OF SPENDING COMPRISING THE FEDERAL BUDGET

Figure 11

CATEGORY	1941	1942	1943	1944	1945	1946	2022	2023
As percentages of outlays:								
Total Outlays	100.0	100.0	100.0	100.0	100.0	100.0	100.0	100.0
National Defense (1)	47.1	73.0	84.9	86.7	89.5	77.3	12.2	13.4
Nondefense:								
Payments for Individuals	18.0	7.0	3.1	2.6	2.6	10.6	72.1	70.7
Direct Payments (2)	15.4	5.8	2.5	2.0	2.0	9.6	59.5	57.3
Grants to State & Local Gov'ts.	2.6	1.2	0.5	0.6	0.5	0.9	12.7	13.4
All Other Grants	3.6	1.4	0.6	0.4	0.4	0.5	6.3	4.3
Net Interest (2)	6.9	3.0	1.9	2.4	3.4	7.4	7.6	10.7
All Other (2)	28.4	18.2	11.0	9.3	5.7	6.8	5.5	3.1
Undistributed Offsetting Receipts (2)	-4.0	-2.5	-1.6	-1.4	-1.5	-2.7	-3.7	-2.2
Total Nondefense	52.9	27.0	15.1	13.3	10.5	22.7	87.8	86.6

(1) INCLUDES A SMALL AMOUT OF GRANTS TO STATE AND LOCAL GOVERNMENTS AND DIRECT PAYMENTS FOR INDIVIDUALS.

(2) INCLUDES SOME OFF-BUDGET AMOUNTS; MOST OF THE OFF-BUDGET AMOUNTS ARE DIRECT PAYMENTS FOR INDIVIDUALS (SOCIAL SECURITY BENEFITS)

DATA FROM "TABLE 6.1—COMPOSITION OF OUTLAYS: 1940–2029," OFFICE OF MANAGEMENT AND BUDGET (OMB), THE WHITE HOUSE, ACCESSED MAY 1, 2024, HTTPS://WWW.WHITEHOUSE.GOV/OMB/BUDGET/HISTORICAL-TABLES/.

The data table above pulls data from the Office of Management and Budget regarding composition of expenditures for 1940–2029, estimated for years 2024–2029. The table is modified to focus on the World War II years of 1941 to 1946, including ramp-up on defense spending in 1941 and ramp-down in 1946. These are compared side by side to 2022 and 2023.

There is a lot to learn from the full time series across 1940 to present, but I want to focus on the comparison of war years to current state. If you look below in the chart of total public debt to GDP ratio, you can see that we are currently at and above WW II levels of indebtedness. The key point here is why? What are we spending the money on? What is the crisis? We've been blowing up the debt since 2009—you might even say since 1981. What is our emergency?

The war years in the table above show the nature of the crisis in clear form for 1941 to 1946; we were saving our country, that of our allies, and all of the world that cared about freedom. Ramped-up, defense spending was never below 73% of congressional outlays and reached as high as 89.5%. We are free because of it. Thank God for the greatest generation.

Now look at the two right hand columns, those shaded for reference. Where is our money now going to incur the same level of indebtedness as it took to win WW II? We are paying bills and benefits to private citizens, along with a few grants and a chunk of interest. What in God's name do we think we are doing? If World War III starts tomorrow, we are in a dire strait of need. That's a genteel way of saying, "We are screwed."

Am I off base here, Working Man? Tell me if you think so. Am I the only one out here thinking this situation is ridiculous? Maybe so. We seem to vote that way.

Let me summarize and repeat for emphasis: We have spent a world war's worth of indebtedness the last several years, and ... there is no war. We are paying bills and benefits to each other. I have a few terms and phrases for this situation: stupid, myopic, dysfunctional, holiday from history, vacation from reality, head in the sand, head in the clouds, head up your behind, catastrophic, unserious, doomed to fail, flippant, unaware, blinkered, callous, devoid of consideration, a black hole of comprehension, unsustainable, no regard for your neighbors and fellow citizens, moronic, prejudged by history as a failure, laughingstock to our enemies, a strategy dreamed up in Beijing or Moscow—and I'm just warming up.

Correct me if you think I'm wrong, Working Man, because I'm telling you, I don't see any way this works. In the name of public benefit, we have obliterated the ability of the federal government to provide the highest-priority public good that the feds are tasked with—national defense. Think of it this way: What good is a financial benefit stream funded by your neighbors if we are overtaken by our enemies? If we lose the next war, of what value is that direct payment?

Life is not without trade-offs. "There is no free lunch," as we like to say in economics. Okay, let's get back to our main text and figure a way out of this mess.

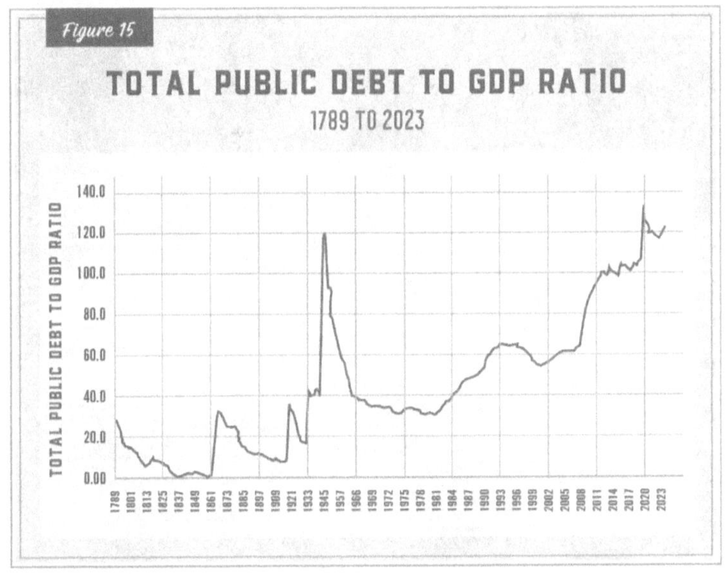

DATA FROM "FEDERAL DEBT TO GDP," LONGTERMTRENDS, ACCESSED APRIL 24, 2024, HTTPS://WWW.LONGTERMTRENDS.NET/US-DEBT-TO-GDP/.

The chart above is sourced from Longtermtrends, showing total U.S. debt to GDP ratios from December 1789 to September 2023. You can see the spike in 1946. Yes, Working Man, as you know, that is World War II. You see that we had no debt anywhere near that level since the adoption of our Constitution. As stated in the main text, I don't think anyone would argue against the investment. And we paid it down, steadily, until the early to mid-1980s. Then our addiction began. You can also see what has happened since late 2008. With respect to addiction, crackheads have nothing on us. We've soared past WWII levels, peaking at 133% in March 2020 with the COVID emergency funds. We've struggled to stay near WWII levels since then. I have to say it again: it's time for a change.

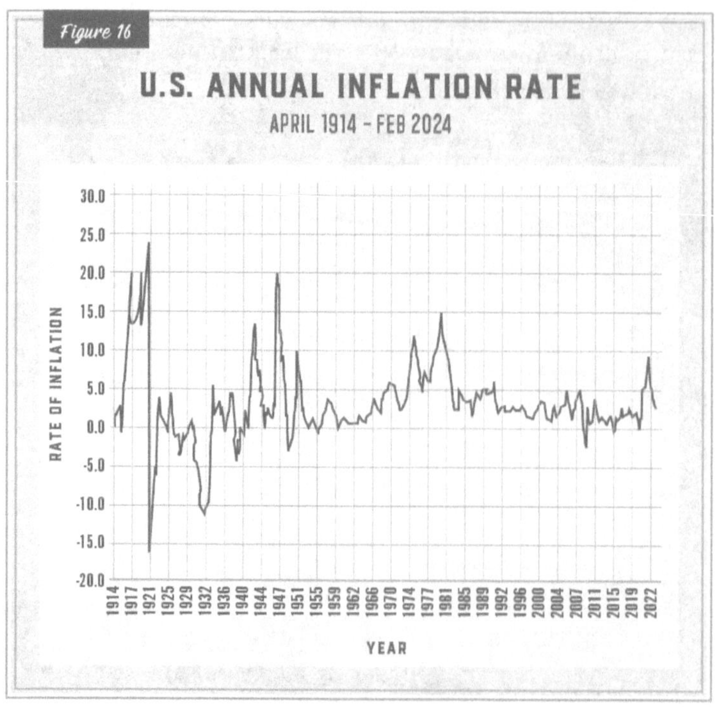

DATA FROM "HISTORICAL INFLATION RATES: 1914-2024," U.S. INFLATION CALCULATOR, COINNEWS MEDIA GROUP, ACCESSED APRIL 24, 2024, HTTPS://WWW. USINFLATIONCALCULATOR.COM/INFLATION/HISTORICAL-INFLATION-RATES/.

The chart above shows the annual rate of inflation, measured monthly from January 1, 1914, through February 1, 2024. The high rates from 1972 to 1980 coincide to the phase known as stagflation. Paul Volcker and Ronald Reagan brought this down by mid-1982, bringing general prosperity to the United States and, correspondingly, to economies across the globe.

As you look at this time series, Working Man, it should be obvious how unnecessary the spike in inflation in recent times has been. The sharp rise in early 2021 was a self-inflicted wound brought about by poor fiscal policy. The "government stimulus" package pushed by the Biden administration, justified by politicians on the basis of the COVID emergency, has been the cause. Bad policy brings bad results. Remember that as you build your legacy, especially when you are standing in the voting booth.

		Figure 17

ANNUAL HOUSEHOLD INCOME IN THE U.S.
UNITED STATES CENSUS BUREAU, 1967–2022

YEAR	CURRENT DOLLARS	CPI ADJUSTED	PRIOR ADJUSTMENT METHOD	ALTERNATIVE ADUSTMENT METHOD
2022	74,580	74,580	74,580	74,580
2012	51,020	63,350	65,340	63,350
2002	42,410	65,820	69,370	65,820
1992	30,640	59,210	62,980	57,320
1982	20,170	55,470	59,010	53,410
1972	9,697	57,170	60,910	54,060
1967	7,143	51,570	54,940	48,780

DATA FROM GLORIA GUZMAN AND MELISSA KOLLAR, "TABLE C-1: HISTORICAL MEDIAN INCOME USING ALTERNATIVE PRICE INDICES 1967–2022," IN *INCOME IN THE UNITED STATES: 2022*, UNITED STATES CENSUS BUREAU, SEPTEMBER 12, 2023, HTTPS:// WWW.CENSUS.GOV/DATA/TABLES/2023/DEMO/INCOME-POVERTY/P60-279.HTML.

I've taken the full time series from the Census Bureau table referenced above for 1967–2022 and focused on a few select years, every decade plus 1967. This is annual median household income. I want to highlight a few items regarding inflation. The full, original table at the website above is full of documentation, footnotes, and explanations. I recommend visiting the site for in-depth use or understanding. I have a simpler purpose here.

Working Man, let's have a quick tutorial on inflation and how to adjust for it. First, look at the column Current Dollars, listed right next to the year. This represents actual, or nominal, dollars measured. Notice the annual income reported for 1967 at $7,143. Now, look at 2022: $74,580. Pretty impressive, eh? The working household did very well with an increase of about $67,000. Not so fast. Your purchasing power from 1967 to 2022 has increased substantially less than $67,000.

The third column, CPI Adjusted, shows income adjusted for inflation using the current method employed by the Census Bureau staff. The price index will place everything in dollars relative to a base year, in this case 2022. In 1967, a certain bundle of goods could be purchased with your income of $7,143.

Fast-forward to 2022, and it takes $51,570 to purchase that same bundle of goods. That's right, Working Man, about $44,000, the difference in column 2 and column 3 for 1967, are gains in wages that mean nothing, eaten up by inflation.

Real, inflation-adjusted gains in wages have occurred between 1967 and 2022, but look at column 3 to measure them, not column 2. The real wage gains are the difference in $51,570 and $74,580, about $23,000. That's a good thing, but you can see the erosive power of inflation. Inflation destroyed about two-thirds of the cash gains from 1967 to 2022. As I've said, it's a devil.

Here's another point of interest. Look at the two right-most columns. Column 4, Prior Adjustment Method, is the price index used by the Census Bureau in times past, prior to the current method. Column 5, Alternative Adjustment Method, is a different price index altogether. Refer to the website for details on index-calculation methods.

The point is that there is more than one method of calculating inflation, and each gives a different outcome. The purpose is the same: to take a bundle of goods and maintain a stable cost (value) over time so that purchasing power can be tracked, but empirical methods can vary.

Take 1967 as an example. Look across the 1967 row to the right, in particular at columns 3, 4, and 5. The difference in income reported is strictly due to different methods of calculating the price index. It can give you a swing of almost $3,000 either way.

Economists and statisticians like myself fret over things like that. For the regular citizen, just make sure your numbers are adjusted by an accepted price index. Don't use current, or nominal, dollars when comparing over time. A politician loves for you to make that mistake. Don't indulge them.

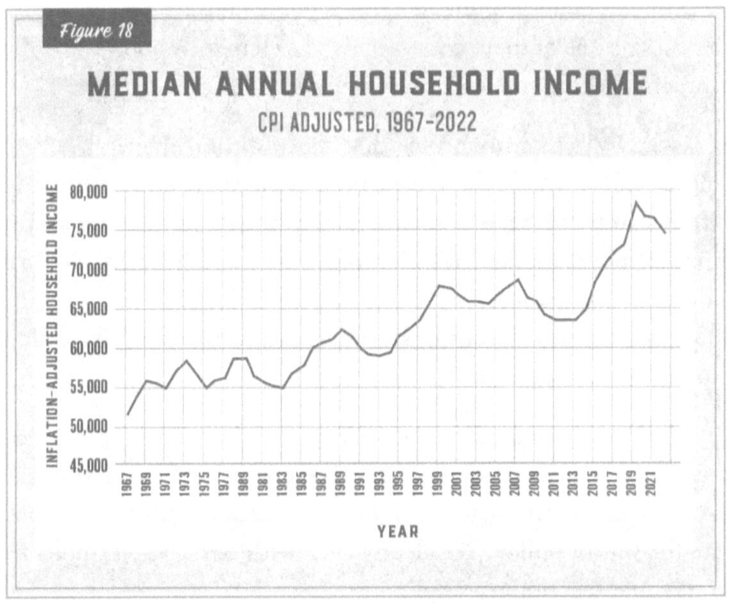

DATA FROM GLORIA GUZMAN AND MELISSA KOLLAR, "TABLE C-1: HISTORICAL MEDIAN INCOME USING ALTERNATIVE PRICE INDICES 1967–2022," IN *INCOME IN THE UNITED STATES: 2022*, UNITED STATES CENSUS BUREAU, SEPTEMBER 12, 2023, HTTPS:// WWW.CENSUS.GOV/DATA/TABLES/2023/DEMO/INCOME-POVERTY/P60-279.HTML.

The chart above is also based on the U.S. Census Bureau Table C-1. I've charted the full time series for the CPI-adjusted annual median household income, 1967 to 2022. This is your purchasing power, Working Man, real, inflation-adjusted dollars, with 2022 as the base. If you want to track quality-of-life metrics, I suggest using monthly household income. I'm using annual here to make certain points over a time span. Monthly numbers get a little crowded for that. Annual works well.

We could rest here a long time and discuss many topics, just looking at the chart above. There are fascinating stories in each and every data point, with dependencies on policies, actions, and events embedded throughout. I'm going to focus on just a few.

Notice those dips along the timeline, going from left to right? Those are drops in quality of life, decreases in purchasing power. Almost every single one of them corresponds to a change in political administrations. People vote with their pocket books in a big way.

And you will certainly notice that sharp dip on the right, beginning in 2019. That's the recent bout with aggregate demand inflation that we've been discussing, Working Man, with a looming threat of bond market inflation darkening the horizon. Will the Biden administration survive this? We will find out in November 2024. They most certainly do not deserve to. They have done enough damage, thank you very much.

The chart above makes our point very clearly regarding inflation. It is your enemy. Recognize this, treat it as such, and vote that way. I long for the day when we, as a nation, think ahead and vote for sound policy. We clearly vote with our pocket books but largely in a reactionary way.

Always and forever reacting to circumstance isn't necessary or optimal. It isn't the best way to live. The policies that give us sound money are known, available, dependable, and stable, no matter the circumstance. Politicians lie, but policies don't. We can think ahead, evaluate with understanding, and demand sound money policies from every administration at all times.

I'll give you an example, Working Man. You've heard these phrases in recent years: "We can print all the money we need," or "The national debt is not relevant." These statements are ridiculous, in any environment. Just run out the logic. If these ideas are true, why do we pay federal tax at all? Eliminate federal income taxes entirely, and put all federal spending on the national credit card. These ideas are garbage, and leftists know this. They don't want to face reality because reality is not in their favor.

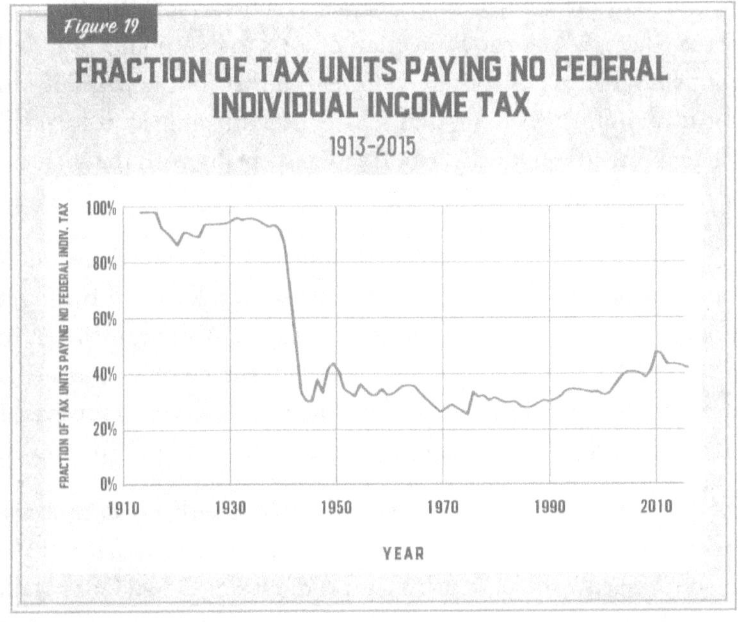

DATA FROM: DAVID SPLINTER, "WHO PAYS NO TAX? THE DECLINING FRACTION PAYING INCOME TAXES AND INCREASING TAX PROGRESSIVITY," *CONTEMPORARY ECONOMIC POLICY* 37, NO. 3 (JULY 2019): 413–26, HTTPS://DOI.ORG/10.1111/COEP.12407.

The chart above is borrowed from David Splinter's article "Who Pays No Tax?" Splinter does excellent work grinding through the intricacies of tax returns. I highly recommend reading his research piece.

The chart shows fractions of "tax units" paying no federal tax. Per Splinter, "Tax units are the conventional unit of observation in tax return data and combine individuals filing a tax return together or who would file together in the case of nonfilers."[98] Of course, "working-age adults" is the number most people think of when discussing how many do or don't pay tax. After thorough detail in converting from tax units to working-age adults, Splinter reduces that far right observation in the chart for 2015, which is about 42%, to 36% for working-age adults.

Other estimates get us to 47%, or 43%, or 50%, or 29.5%, numbers cited in the references of Chapter 7, subsection "The Tyranny of the Majority and the Protection of Prosperity," policy proposal number 8. Estimates coming in lower than any of these usually do not account for tax credits and rebates, looking only at filing data. These numbers are low by a long shot, especially with the increase in tax credits in recent years.

Any way you look at it, there are a bunch of folks out there, all of them voters, paying no federal tax whatsoever. Many of them get money back, direct wealth transfers from one American citizen to another. I begrudge no one for taking advantage of legal benefits on clear offer, Working Man. That's normal behavior. However, I do call us back to that most basic of economic concepts: incentives.

If I stand in a voting booth and bequeath myself benefits at the expense of others, can we deem ourselves to be a serious nation? We must reconsider. I would ask a simple question: Do you ever walk through the cash register checkout line at Costco, only to turn and ask the person behind you to pay your bill? I've never a single time in my life seen that happen, at any register in any store in the entire country. But if you place us in a voting booth, we think differently.

I honestly believe we should stop that habit. Incentives have created this habit, a habit that is not sustainable, and those incentives can be changed. May it happen soon.

---

[98]   Splinter, "Who Pays No Tax?"

LET'S KEEP THE
CONVERSATION
going

Visit **https://aworkingmansguide.com** to get more values-driven content right to your inbox.

Order special bulk purchases for your company, organization, or community by contacting **teaguesix@yahoo.com**.

Book Dr. Mark L. Teague for speaking and consultations via **https://aworkingmansguide.com**.

CONNECT WITH **DR. MARK L. TEAGUE**

Facebook: DrMarkLTeague

Instagram: @DrMarkLTeague

X: @DrMarkLTeague

LinkedIn: DrMarkLTeague

Thank you
FOR READING!

If you enjoyed *A Working Man's Guide,* please leave a review on Goodreads or on the retailer site where you purchased this book and help me reach more readers like you.

www.ingramcontent.com/pod-product-compliance
Lightning Source LLC
Chambersburg PA
CBHW031540150726
47990CB00001B/247